Volume Practice I

Volume Practice I

A Chiropractor's Success Story

**Thomas Outler Morgan, B.S., D.C.
with Mary Ann (Kalb) Morgan, B.A.**

CONTACT: thomasoutlermorgan1942@gmail.com

E-BookTime, LLC
Montgomery, Alabama

Volume Practice I

A Chiropractor's Success Story

Copyright © 1991 by Thomas Outler Morgan, B.S., D.C.

ISBN: 978-1-60862-809-4

First Printing: 1991
Second Printing: 1992
Third Printing: 1997
Fourth Printing: 2021

E-BookTime, LLC
6598 Pumpkin Road
Montgomery, AL 36108
www.e-booktime.com

ACKNOWLEDGEMENTS

This book is dedicated to chiropractic children. Like us, they move as seemingly immortal units in their youth. Later, like all of us, they learn who they belong to, and that they must face the mortal enemy. Even so, my faith is for them to carry on our great science – chiropractic – and to keep it separate and distinct from allopathy.

I want to thank my wife, Mary Ann, who not only edited and corrected this manuscript, but who always urged me on and who has never lost faith in me.

I want to further comment on two facts which are self evident in these pages. First of all, I believe that Jesus Christ is the son of God, and the savior of the world. I was unable to keep the writing strictly secular, so if you are reading this book, and are not a Christian, please try to indulge me. Next, although I sometimes refer only to the male genre at times in this book, let me assure you that I mean no disrespect. Indeed, I have great respect for the female doctors in the field. Our daughter Dr. Amy is a great chiropractor and her oldest daughter Hannah, is currently in chiropractic college.

PREFACE

I want you to study this book, for herein lie some secrets you can use to become the greatest chiropractor you want to become. I want to tell you how to attract patients whom you can really help, to your clinic. Also, I want to give you some direction in life, which you can use to reach the highest mountain you can climb. I believe that everyone has a mountain which they can reach, which is even beyond their own comprehension.

There is a potential within you for greatness. Remember that great people are just average people who are in a position to do great things and have the ability to commit themselves to the task at hand. Right now you are in a position to help hundreds and thousands of sick and suffering people, right where you are. There are people walking by your office who need and want to know how to eliminate the fear of disease and how to have faith in a healing system which does not depend on doctors or treatments.

The purpose of this book is to help you become free of fear. It will help you overcome the fear of being incomplete in this life, fear of yourself, and your inadequacies, fear of commitment. It can help you with this commitment, and you can go forward with ideas and actions which benefit mankind and glorify God. I feel that you can overcome fear and become the chiropractor and person you were destined to become when you decided to attend chiropractic college. I believe that chiropractors are special in this world. No one has the training that we do, nor the understanding to lead people into an understanding of health, not sickness. Come with me through these pages, as I attempt to tell you what it was that brought sixty-two new patients to my office on an average working day. Come, let me tell you what I think about each day, and what it took to get myself into the position to adjust over one thousand, two hundred patients per week for several years. This was our average from 1970 to 1973. Most importantly, I hope to be able to relate to you why it was necessary for me and for you to have such an era in our lives, to learn from and to understand. Let us begin together, and share our understanding.

T. O. Morgan, B.S., D.C.

Contents

PART I

Section 3

Section 4

Section 5

PART II

Section 1

Section 2

Section 3

Section 4

Section 5

Part I

A CHIROPRACTOR'S SUCCESS STORY

PROLOGUE

I was practicing in Verona, Mississippi (population 3,000) in April of 1972, that memorable year when one of the greatest achievements of my life was accomplished. I was nearly twenty-nine years old. I remember that around 10:00 on that Wednesday evening, I walked up front to the receptionists' desk. Mary Ann, my wife, and three other assistants were studying the sign-in sheet. Three hundred and ninety-eight patients had signed in that day. Just then, the door opened, and a husband and wife came in and registered. That made four hundred patients I had adjusted that day! Office hours began at 7:30 that morning, and we had worked straight through with only a very short lunch break. Dr. Bob Goodwin, a young chiropractor who was the exam doctor at that time, witnessed this record, which was unheard of at the time.

When I was driving home that night, I felt the usual heaviness in my legs and the puffiness in my hands. I said my usual prayer in the car and wondered if I would ever be able to tell new chiropractors what it cost in dedication, time and stamina to get in a position where four hundred people would come into your clinic in one day to get adjusted. Was there some magical secret to this phenomenal success? I did not know that many chiropractors would be upset because of this volume practice – certainly the patients did not complain. However, later there were innuendoes about my "not doing the patients justice" and "not spending sufficient time with each patient." I learned a lot about success with a volume practice and a lot about chiropractors.

Later I flew my plane to Davenport, Iowa, to speak to two hundred students. I found that there was only eagerness to learn about how and why this had happened to me. I was asked to speak in many states, and everywhere I went people wanted to know about my office procedures, such as what I said to people and what my particular technique was. These students believed that it was something that one could see or demonstrate that was responsible for my great success. Very few wanted to hear about how many hours it took to see an average of one thousand, two hundred patients per week. No one wanted to know about the sacrifices Mary Ann and our children endured for me to accomplish this achievement.

Everyone wanted to know how I was doing and what I was doing. Not everyone had complimentary things to say, however. Some said that I was obsessed, insane, and unprofessional. I was told that I was "cheapening" the profession, and some detractors claimed that I was not doing the chiropractic profession justice. I was doing something which had never been done before, and I would like to relate to you what it took to get into this position of service. You see, I believe that it is the highest privilege on earth to be able to lose yourself in service to people through the greatest healing profession known to man.

BORN TO VOLUME

"DO NOT PRAY FOR EASIER LIVES. ASK TO BE STRONGER MEN. DO NOT ASK FOR TASKS THAT ARE EQUAL TO YOUR STRENGTH. ASK FOR STRENGTH EQUAL TO YOUR TASKS."
Phillips Brooks

How can a doctor, with the endless details of patient influencing, diagnosis, and care, be free to adjust hundreds of patients daily? The answer lies in the esoterics of the doctor-patient relationship. I was led to experience this truth first-hand one day when I was a senior at Palmer College of Chiropractic in Davenport, Iowa. In the frat house one afternoon I answered the phone. Instead of the usual woman seeking the Delta Sigma Chi brother of her dreams, it was Mrs. Frank Bemis, Sr. from Alton, Illinois. Her husband, a chiropractor, had been called out of town because his father was near death in New York. Since it was such a sudden departure for him, there was no time to contact all the patients who were scheduled for the following day. Mrs. Bemis was looking for a senior student who could come down and work for a few days until Dr. Bemis's return. I jumped at the chance! Neither she nor I gave much thought about the legality of my not having a diploma or an Illinois license, but that is another story! I jumped in my old Ford and took off for Alton.

Mrs. Bemis met me at the office which was on the main street of town. She did not tell me how many patients were scheduled, but Dr. Bemis normally saw more than one hundred visits per day. I looked over the adjusting table and proceeded to use my vast mechanical knowledge to figure out how the thing worked! Finally, I called Dr. Bemis in New York and he talked me through his equipment and technique. I felt blindly positive that I was indeed the GREAT chiropractor needed for the job! The Hi-Lo was all hydraulic, and although I cannot remember the name of the table, I know that we did not have one like it at Palmer. I do remember, though, that all the sections moved prolifically forward and backward in many adjustable positions, but they did not drop like those on the Thompson table on which I was trained.

The next morning, Mrs. Bemis got me up at 6:00 and insisted on feeding me. Usually I never ate until noon, but she assured me that I would need my strength! I adjusted seventy patients that day stopping only long enough to have a sandwich for lunch. At 7:00 p.m., I had to drag myself to the car. When I got to the Bemises' house, I could not even eat (something very unusual for me). The only things I wanted were a shower and sleep. My first lesson was that you have to be in shape in order to handle a volume practice. The next morning though, I was raring to go. However, when we got to the office, we started receiving phone calls from local chiropractors who threatened to turn me into the Board of Examiners if I did not leave town. I left on this note, but not without great admiration for a doctor whom I would not meet until much later, a positive chiropractic wife (I hoped to marry a woman just like Mrs. Bemis some day), and most of all, the unique opportunity to work a volume practice with the most loving patients I could ever imagine.

There were only two mishaps. One happened when a patient allowed her feet to hang over the footplate on the adjusting table. When the table was lowered, the footplate would come flush with the floor. I can still hear the "CRUNCH" her toes made when the table came down on them. Her toes were bleeding, and I began to fumble through the desk to find something with which to bandage them. She never said a word but smiled and finally commented on the nice job I did bandaging her toes. The second mishap was when I tried to use the wrong cuff to take a patient's blood pressure. There was only one patient who wanted me to take her blood pressure. So, being highly trained in the art and use of the sphygmomanometer, I found this cuff and proceeded to pump it up. There was no bulb to pump with, so I searched and finally found a bulb. It was too big, but I held it tightly with my other hand and tried to pump it up anyway. I pumped and pumped, but I could never get it to go past 100 mmHg! The patient just smiled and looked at me sweetly. Finally I asked her what her blood pressure reading normally was. When she told me, I looked her squarely in the eye and said, "Well, it's the same today!"

I also worked with Dr. Joseph Kehoe during my last year at Palmer. Joe taught me a lot about volume practice. However, it was my visit with Dr. John Blossom in Montpelier, Ohio that really gave me the vision of the far. There will be more about John later.

GETTING PREPARED

"THE PHILOSOPHY WHICH IS SO IMPORTANT IN EACH OF US IS NOT A TECHNICAL MATTER; IT IS OUR MORE OR LESS DUMB SENSE OF WHAT LIFE HONESTLY AND DEEPLY MEANS. IT IS ONLY PARTLY GOT FROM BOOKS; IT IS OUR INDIVIDUAL WAY OF JUST SEEING AND FEELING THE TOTAL PUSH AND PRESSURE OF THE COSMOS."
John Locke

I recall Dr. Galen Price explaining the major premises of chiropractic during a philosophy class in my first quarter at Palmer in old classroom 201. At the time, I wondered what this was all about. One thing rang through clearly: every teacher wove the thread of chiropractic into the teaching at Palmer. We could identify with these teachers as people who had a new approach to health care; people who used no drugs and who only wanted to help patients. This central theme was so different from that of a regular college curriculum, since it seemed that Palmer wanted to make a chiropractor out of me! I was very impressed with the teaching staffs' dedication to chiropractic and to teaching.

I was, and still am, amazed that the body can completely change with only one adjustment, that simply moving a vertebra into position can create wholeness where once there was only sickness and despair. I enjoyed all of the basic sciences, but the chiropractic sciences, especially the technique courses, held a special attraction for me. I intended to become a better adjuster than anyone else in my class. I also had the largest clinic practice in the student clinic. These were the first two goals that I made up my mind to achieve.

The chiropractic philosophy of Innate Intelligence captivated my mind at Palmer. The teaching and philosophizing among the students was so interesting that I became more and more intrigued. In fact, when I came home from chiropractic school and saw my friends doing the same things we had always done in high school, I knew that I was different now and that I knew something which none of them knew. This knowledge served to increase my faith and belief in chiropractic's natural system of healing.

In my senior year at Palmer, I began to think seriously about the practice-building courses available to those in the profession. People from the Clinic Masters program were coming on campus to promote their program. Representatives from other groups, called chiropractic specialists, were giving their lectures off campus. I wanted to try my own way of practicing, but soon after graduation, my best friend, David Hughes, convinced me not to "try and reinvent the wheel," but rather to go to Texas with him because everyone said that the Parker Management Course was THE practice management system to use. We went, and I really liked the first night because Dr. Jim Parker talked about the pioneer spirit and the need for chiropractic. Dr. Parker taught us every word of his textbook and saved me from making a lot of mistakes. I have a lot of respect for him. He taught hundreds of us the procedures by which to better serve patients. David and I went to the Parker seminar four times. I credit Dr. Parker with the fact that I had a positive cash flow from my very first month in practice. I believe he still guarantees "no starvation period" with his system.

A few months later, David called and said that we were going to Atlanta to the Dynamic Essential (D.E.) meeting. Just a few days prior to this decision, I had received a small card in the mail with the letters "D.E." on it, but I had no idea what it meant. David picked me up in his Volkswagen, and we attended the third D.E. meeting ever held. There was no textbook, only a yellow legal pad for each doctor present. Dr. Sid Williams talked for four days about the dynamic essential of a volume chiropractic practice. As he talked, I wrote down his famous words, "I accept all cases, regardless of condition or financial ability to pay." We were taught how to advertise free X-rays and sent home with the charge to adjust as many people as possible in one day. I did not doubt or question any of the ideas which this man propounded. I felt like he was trying to revive the catalyst behind B.J. Palmer's central theme "The Big Idea." I went home with enthusiasm and began to put what I had learned into practice.

THE FEELING

"CONFIDENCE IS THE FEELING YOU HAVE, JUST BEFORE YOU FULLY UNDERSTAND THE SITUATION."
Unknown

I want to tell you how I felt when I first opened my office in Warsaw, Kentucky. I was so enthusiastic to tell people about chiropractic (and I wanted to adjust them) that I developed the now famous system that I had taught at the D.E. Meetings for many years called the "Touch and Tell" system. When I first got into practice, I instructed my receptionist to tell everyone who came in the front door, not to tell the doctor what was wrong with them. Instead, she would tell the new patients that the doctor had a method of testing the nerves whereby he could tell them what was wrong, rather than them telling him. I have examined thousands of spines, and with each subluxation, I have programmed my "cranial software" to store up information about the symptoms and characteristics of each subluxation. Eventually, I could tell a patient what symptoms each subluxation was causing, how the symptom was acting, and how I could help them to get over it. Pretty soon the word spread in the small town where I was practicing that the new doctor was a "mind reader." I simply told them that I was a "spine reader!" I was so anxious to try out the adjustment on patients with organic conditions and "incurable" conditions that I told everyone to urge these people to come in. If I did not help them, they would not have to pay me. I was only charging $4.00 for an adjustment in 1964, and we would get most people to pay $32.00

in advance for ten adjustments. I have always believed that if I can get the patient to come in ten times, I can accomplish three major objectives: to clear them out and get them better, to tell them about the Big Idea, and to get their families to come in with them. In the beginning, I felt that nothing could stop me. I was twenty-three years old then and ready to heal the world. I built my practice to fifty patients per day then and felt that it was all I could ever see in one day. Eventually, after altering my system I found that I could see one hundred patients per day without much problem. My office in Kentucky had only one adjusting room, and I believed that with more room and more tables, I could do far more adjusting.

A VISION OF THE FAR

"GENIUS IS ONE PERCENT INSPIRATION AND NINETY-NINE PERCENT PERSPIRATION."
Unknown

After I had been in practice in Kentucky for about six months, I went to Montpelier, Ohio to visit Dr. John Blossom, who was using a system which his father had taught him. He had two adjusting rooms with five tables in each room, and he would have five women in one room and five men in the other. I watched him adjust sixty-seven patients in four hours one evening, and I was very impressed. When I designed my clinic in Mississippi in 1969, I had four large adjusting rooms built so that I could use this system too, but I changed it somewhat. I could put six patients in each room, but I only used one adjusting table per room. My patients would sit on benches while waiting in line to get on the table, and as soon as the adjustment was completed, they would carry their records out to the front desk. Soon I was having twenty-four patients waiting in the adjusting rooms, fifteen patients in the waiting room several new patients in either examination room or the X-ray room. Everyone who ever watched me adjust a couple hundred patients in one day never forgot what they saw. It was truly a wonderful time in my life, and I felt blessed to be able to do this work. It made me want to help other D.C.s to be able to do this same kind of service and to have successful practices.

YOUR SPINE, THE KEY TO HEALTH

"GOD WILL ALWAYS REVEAL HIS WILL TO ONE WHO IS WILLING TO DO IT."
Unknown

First you must have a "flag." This should be the very first thing you decide before opening up your office. When I was growing up in northern Kentucky, I would drive up and down the Dixie Highway through Covington. At one particular sharp curve was a chiropractor's office, and I would slow down to look at it. The chiropractor who was practicing in a house by this curve had a large human spine painted on his chimney with the words "Your Spine, The Key To Health." I looked at that spine every time we drove to Covington. I did not know anything about chiropractic, nor was there ever any mention of it in health or more appropriately "sickness" classes in high school. It was not until a few years later that I was befriended by Bill King and was introduced to his father, the famous Dr. James N. King, who was the chiropractor with the spine painted on his chimney. The fact that I noticed the spine on the chimney before I ever knew about chiropractic convinced me of the importance of a "flag" – an eye catcher that would announce the presence of chiropractic to the world. To this day, I bet there is not a single person who grew up in northern Kentucky when I did who does not remember the spine on the chimney, even though they still may not know about the benefits of chiropractic care.

When I opened my office in Verona, Mississippi, I had an eight-foot sign made just like the one on Dr. King's chimney, and it hung in my parking lot for many, many years. I suggest that the name you give your clinic and the theme of your public relations programs reflect what you are and what you want your community to think about you as their doctor.

HEALING FUNDAMENTALS FOR CHIROPRACTORS

"DON'T LET THE FUTURE BE THAT TIME WHEN YOU WISH YOU'D DONE WHAT YOU AREN'T DOING NOW."

There is a process of thinking which can govern your actions and make them either positive or negative. How you function in your daily routine is controlled by your thoughts, not your environment. Many world leaders know how to think creatively and positively, as well as how to tune into God's energy which governs the universe. These people, however, cannot control your thoughts or actions unless you let them. They have an inner energy that stems from positive thoughts which allows them to carry themselves with authority to accomplish their goals and to be effective leaders in their space in their time. You must do the same, wherever you are.

While it may be true that we all live in the same world, there are great differences in our thought processes. If you can see the completion of a task with your inner mind, keep it secret, believe it to be possible, and tune into the divine energy which is available to everyone, there can be no reason for it not to be forthcoming, if your secret thoughts agree with natural and spiritual law. Some things that defy even natural laws are made possible by an innate spiritual strength. For example, scientists cannot explain the World War II Spitfires which returned across the English Channel and landed safely. When the ground crew looked inside the planes, they found that the pilots had been dead for as long as an hour! It is my personal belief that someone was holding a positive thought. This thought was held secretly in accordance with divine law, because these planes were desperately needed by the British in the war effort. The person or persons who held this secret thought evidently knew how to tap the endless universal energy, and God landed the planes safely without the benefit of human guidance. You do not have to be "good" or "evil" in order to tap into this energy. You must only be capable of understanding how to do it. All of us have similar stories in our lives, which seem almost too bizarre to mention. These happenings were made possible by a creative mind process, unidentified by science. Let us take at look at how this works in chiropractic.

Gravity is a natural law that has been used to explain a universal law over which we seemingly have no control. This law was discovered by Sir Isaac Newton, who used the example of an apple falling off the tree, and this same "apple theory" has often been used to describe the way chiropractic works. The apple always falls to the ground unless it is impeded somewhere along the way. Let us compare this law with the chiropractic law which states that the power always flows from above down, inside out, unless there is an impediment along the way (subluxation). Just as you can "hold" the apple in the air in your mind, so too can the subluxation stop the flow of divine energy from reaching vital organs. The patients themselves may even be giving this subluxation more power by holding negative or "sick" thoughts, thereby increasing their sickness. The chiropractor, on the other hand, can remove the subluxation as well as develop a belief system by which he lives that can only add positivity to the healing process. In order to do this, you must realize that your thoughts need discipline.

We have all dealt with people who do not want to be better. What do we, as doctors, do when our patients only want us to control their symptoms or conditions? The answer lies in the thought process, which is held secretly in the mind of the doctor and agrees with natural and spiritual law. The answer does not lie in explanations or treatments, but rather in the removal of subluxations. With the chiropractor's being able to actually tune into the patient's Innate Intelligence with his own mind, he can increase the body's will to be well. It is our job, then, not only to adjust, but to mentally remove the interference with this power and then let the natural and spiritual forces do the rest, regardless of the temporarily misguided mind of the patient. The result of this is that the patient feel changed mechanically as well as inwardly.

Chiropractors add nothing to the body, nor do they take anything away. Rather, we concentrate on the healing process itself. We strive for an Innate bonding which dissipates the conscious negativity brought about by the "fear" programming of the medical world. When results are positive, the patient then becomes open to changing his health concepts and begins thinking of preventive chiropractic care. This is challenged when the patient's child has a fever or symptom. When the patient does not respond to your adjustments, it is your duty to refer to another D.C. for care. Since each of us is different, the bonding is also different. This difference is brought to the surface by understanding the anatomical differences in our hands as well as the differences in the mental process thus making every D.C.'s technique distinct. The "sick" thoughts of the patients cannot be "blamed" for not achieving results. The key that keeps me in tune to this principle is to give ALL the credit to Innate and to give thanks that I was an instrument through which Innate Intelligence was released and homeostasis restored.

THE PRINCIPLE

"THE MEN OF PRINCIPLE ARE THE PRINCIPAL MEN."
B. J. Palmer

This epigram sprang forth to all of us throughout our years at Palmer College of Chiropractic. B.J. spent his early days in chiropractic doing much research, but in the late 1920s, he seemed to turn to a technique era unsurpassed before or since that time. This era was marked by the "Hole in One" (HIO) technique where chiropractors gave specific adjustments to ONLY the atlas and the axis. In 1960, when I enrolled at Palmer, Dr. P.A. Remier was still looking at stereo upper cervical plates, and every student got an appointment to discuss his X-rays with Dr. P.A. I remember P.A. well. He looked exactly like his picture in his X-ray book. His office smelled somewhere between bourbon and tobacco, and there were volumes of X-rays lined along the walls. During my appointment, Dr. P.A. only discussed the occipital atlantal-axis area and pointed out the rotation I had at the atlas. I remember him saying that my neck would not give me much trouble, as there was a good lordosis and very little atlas laterality involved. Also, I was a "constant" (C1 and C2 were both rotated right). He drew the lines, marked ASRA on the film, shook my hand, and told me to enjoy my stay at Palmer.

The word "principled" comes directly from the mouths of straight chiropractors. This term meant that you believed in the Innate principle of healing so vital to chiropractic, plus you were a principled chiropractor – a principled man. I did not know that this was such a dynamic play on words to anchor one to straight chiropractic or to focus this supremacy attitude against everyone who did not agree with us straights. We set ourselves apart as strong, principled, straight chiropractors – acting as if we had secret knowledge about Innate Intelligence. I see this today as a separatist attitude which has held the profession back in many ways.

I was always intrigued with the natural healing phenomenon involved with the adjustment. D.D. Palmer was not the first person to move a spinal vertebra by hand in order to help a sick person. What Palmer did was to connect the neurology to the subluxation phenomenon and to thereby postulate the "Palmer Law of Life." He was the first to state the fact that Innate Intelligence resides in the body's nervous system and is interfered with by osseous barriers at the spinal level. The specific chiropractic adjustment corrects the alignment problem, but the healing mechanism is a natural physical function of repair and regeneration under the control of Innate. For the first time in health care, Palmer based his new science on health and where it comes from, rather than on a disease process or sickness and its subsequent treatment or treatments (medicine). A fifth point was hence added to the health picture, i.e.:

1. Diet
2. Rest
3. Exercise
4. Positive mental attitude (stress)
5. A properly functioning nervous system (no osseous interference)

I believe the goal of the chiropractor is to expect the patient to function normally following the adjustment. This homeostasis is the main goal of lifetime chiropractic. This principle was true in 1895 and it is still true today. Einstein knew the atom had been available for six thousand years. He cracked this scientific phenomenon and changed physics and the world forever. Like Innate, the power of the atom was always there. However, it was never understood in the way in which Einstein understood it.

Likewise, the spinal adjustment was not new, but the adjustment PLUS the explanation of the self-healing mechanism of Innate Intelligence was first hypothesized by D.D. Palmer. From that point on, this new kind of doctor would not add nor take anything away from the body to establish health. The adjustment released the life energy already in charge of the body's functions. Palmer knew this healing principle was spiritual in the same way that the force of gravity is spiritual. They both fulfill a part of God's plan for humanity. Without gravity, we would fall off the planet. In the presence of subluxation, without the adjustment, the body becomes a sick and malfunctioning organism. It was a fortunate event that chiropractic was not projected as a religion or as a type of magnetic healing, but rather as a scientific principle which could be duplicated time after time.

B.J. was very wise in the development of chiropractic. He focused his new science on the spine and only the spine. He got the state legislatures to license chiropractors, with the spine and joints as our points of anatomic focus. The profession took off and has grown as a separate and distinct science despite the total boycott and ostracism made by organized medicine. Our phenomenal growth is a credit to the free market. We grew mostly on private schools with a great lack of university backing and public funds. Our growth has also come from the millions of sick people who went to chiropractors when medicine failed to help them, AND THEY GOT WELL!! Our results kept us in the market place. We did the adjusting. Innate did the healing. We served our patients regardless of condition or financial ability to pay. We believed that we were servants of the sick, and we offered them an alternate way of healing and health. We proved the hypothesis with our outstanding clinical results! I am one who believes that B.J. did more for the profession than any chiropractor ever has. I personally believe that the profession as a whole, and research will decide technique and practice parameters for us in the future. Practices in the future will rely on a proven objective belief system, which will make the adjustments faster, more effective and more economical. A united effort could be utilized here. I have now seen communism declared to be a failure and the Berlin Wall has come down without a shot being fired. Perhaps this is the way unity will come to our profession someday. I believe that it will come in much the same manner, by Divine Providence.

REAL SUCCESS

"A WINNER NEVER QUITS AND A QUITTER NEVER WINS."
                              Unknown

It is difficult to gauge your good fortune. If you see lots of sick people, make a lot of money, and have all the worldly amenities you desire, is it because you are just "lucky?" I wonder who first said that "success is 99 percent perspiration and 1 percent inspiration?" Whoever said it was definitely on to something! Luck is sometimes not earned or even expected. This happens to one in a million. The rest of us must plan our work and work our plan.

The catalyst behind the successful person is an innate positive persistence. When one refuses to believe in disappointments and continues to push on inch by inch, there is soon a reward for his efforts.

A doctor who has practiced for a couple of decades must reassess his energy level. To do this, he must keep motivated in his work by setting new goals and by giving his experience to students. These protégés rebound within and keep the energy level up so the doctor can continue to practice day after day. One must follow the advances in chiropractic and incorporate this knowledge into his practice. One of the most important things is to have a very secure financial position so the twilight years in your practice can be more "fun" and patient needs can be fitted into a more limited schedule.

THERE IS NO LUCK – ONLY GRACE

"WINNERS MAKE COMMITMENTS; LOSERS MAKE ALIBIS."
William Harris, D.C.

You often hear of the person who "hits the jackpot" or who answered the question and won thousands of dollars. Was this luck or grace? The world's system wants you to stand amazed at this "luck!" However, I tell you that there is no respect for this occurrence in real life. Real life, the good life, is day after day jobs, with vacations and a happy home and family. My respect is for the chiropractor in the trenches who works long hours, striving for the challenge of the new patient. I have seen many "speakers" in the seminar business who could not sustain the year-in year-out practice schedule. Perhaps one would think that he was too good to care for the ailing Mrs. Jones. I say that the greatest reward needs to be aimed toward the chiropractors who put this profession where it is today. This is the average doctor working with only himself and a few family members and friends who understand the positive ramifications of the adjustment that he has spent his life providing. This doctor also supports his state association, keeps current in technique and refers others into the chiropractic profession.

Yes, I believe that you make your own "luck." You get what you deserve. You spend your entire life overcoming your "self," your rebellion, your laziness, your bad habits, your pride, your arrogance, and your sins.

I also believe in my Lord and savior Jesus Christ. I believe that when you turn your life over to Him, you come home to the power that made you. I believe the Apostle Paul's words that you must be "dead to sin," and as you see your sins abating, you know that it is God releasing the selfish "hunger" out of you. It is God who lets you view your spiritual advance through Him to a point where you definitely know what the Christian life is all about – GRACE. Your undeserved blessings, this GRACE is the only real luck there is. We must be thankful for this great gift from God.

AFFIRMATIONS

"YOUR DESTINY IS DETERMINED BY CHOICE, NOT BY CHANCE."
Unknown

All of us assess our practice, family, goals, wants and desires every day. As you meditate on your daily lives, here are some things to consider in your routine. First, offer adoration to God for everything He has given you. Next, confess all known sins, hatred, bitterness, laziness, apathy, illusions, bad habits, etc. Then focus on your positive goals and aspirations.

Here are some considerations:

- Settle yourself into a relaxed position, prone or sitting.
- Mentally relax your body.
- Stop all thought processes.
- Concentrate on your respiration.
- Start picturing the people you love the most – family, friends, patients, others.
- Begin to be thankful for these people.
- Affirm these people in their state of spiritual advance.
- Affirm them clear of subluxations.
- Affirm them smiling and peaceful, seeking Jesus' embrace.
- Affirm them regenerated by Innate Intelligence.
- Affirm them fulfilling their duties.

- Affirm all material possessions for which you are thankful.
- Affirm all goals on which you are working.
- Affirm your spiritual progress and promotions given by grace.
- Affirm yourself as subluxation-free, healthy, happy, strong, and peaceful.
- Affirm your actions for that day, what needs improvement, what you did well.
- Affirm your actions for tomorrow.
- Affirm God's greatness, His omnipresence, omnipotence.
- Affirm, praise, and worship His holy name – your creator, savior, and comforter.
- Affirm all your family and friends who believe in Jesus Christ being together, because Jesus granted us eternal life.
- Relax or sleep and listen to the Holy Spirit as it gives utterance.

By using these guidelines, you can start losing yourself and the concentration in the above will open channels for God to apply His thoughts to your consciousness. Then write down your goals, thoughts, desires. The secret affirmation is to totally concentrate on what you have, what you want, why you are here, and God's plan and purpose for your life.

THE LAW OF GROWTH

*"ADVERSITY CAUSES SOME PEOPLE TO BREAK DOWN
AND OTHERS TO BREAK RECORDS."*
Unknown

I used to raise a garden when I lived in Mississippi. I bought seed, tilled the soil, and planted the seed. It sounds simple, but my garden never looked very good, nor did it bear well. I began to talk to some of my old patients who had gardens. What I learned from them were the "tricks" to producing a vigorously growing garden that would yield above normal crops. What helped me to pick up on these tips was the fact that I had been trying to garden for a couple of years by reading books and trying out "my" thoughts on planting, etc. When these old boys began to share their secrets with me, and even bring in seed which they had bred for years, then I understood that I would never have the knowledge, under-standing, or dedication to cultivate the kind of garden they had unless I made this one of the supreme work priorities of my life. I could see the dedication in these masterful gar-deners, who fulfilled their final years perfecting their gardens, and they were like skilled consultants helping a new graduate to enter practice. As for me, I went as far as I wanted to go in understanding and growing principles and raised a better garden with my limited interest. My average garden is like an average practice. Without total dedication, you cannot reach a maximum practice. You may not achieve what someone else does, but unless you use what these other people have done, you may negate your own ability, work, and desire.

What counts are the areas where you know deep down that you are an "ordained" doctor and that you are supposed to reach the highest level God wants you to reach. You have to muster every ounce of courage, desire, discipline, knowledge, and tenacity to make this commitment. This is a glory known only by God, your family, and your patients. Remember, do not read your press clippings. Rather, when you succeed give all the credit to God. A wise man once said, "The duties are ours; the credits are God's."

When a farmer stands in his field in January and sees a wet, cold, sour, and desolate field, his mind is on springtime and the next harvest time. He knows that the dead and desolate appearance of the field is only a temporary illusion. He knows that God, in His wisdom, has put "order" to every-thing and that soon the springtime will come again. He has the knowledge and skills to see his field swell with his crop, and the harvest will be bigger and better than ever before. Without understanding the growth principle and without his work and dedication, the field will grow up in weeds and stay useless. Understanding that part of his vision makes you realize that most faith comes from knowledge. The rest comes from hard work. We must see our offices full and our fields white with the harvest.

We have access to senses which can feed God's positive energy to our consciousness. What we perceive with the five senses can affect us positively or negatively. When right, they touch our spirit and the power of their perfection is fed to our consciousness. The routine feeding of our senses can by the catalyst needed for our spiritual advance. In the perception of literature, art and music there is truth. Seek these out each day:

1. Literature – each day read positive, inspired works. The written language has within it perfection and truth. Seek it out, read it, meditate on it and you will receive power. Books of truth can be religious, success oriented, motivational, or classics. My personal recommendation would include a daily Bible reading along with other material. Scripture reflects the mind of God, and we must know God's mind in order to do His will. It is okay to read recreational literature for pleasure, but make sure that these books leave you with a good feeling. I personally like to read several different books at a time.

2. Art – what you see can create positive, beautiful thoughts that can feed your consciousness into the state of perfection. A real-life picture of nature's beauty, such as a tree, a countryside, a plant, an insect, or an animal can be truly inspiring. There is one hundred per cent pure talent in a picture. Look for it and meditate on the creative talent that God gives some of his creatures. The great artists can recreate their thoughts on canvas. Try to tune into this, and it can give you faith and power.

3. Music – the sense of hearing can bring violence or peace. It is in all sound and how it is perceived by you. Listen each day to pure inspired music. There can be happiness and hope in sounds, particularly the sound of music filled with love and power. Learn to speak from a position of love. This openness is the key to accepting all people and patients, regardless of who they are, what they look like, or what they have. That way every patient is treated as if he were part of your very own family.

The other senses can be used as a discipline each day, but start with the three above. Concentrate on filling each sense with the pure vibrations that can help you rise above a world bent on wallowing in the catastrophes of the six o'clock news.

GETTING STARTED

"FAITH IS DARING TO DO SOMETHING REGARDLESS OF THE CONSEQUENCES."

You must get started. You must begin today. A preventive conscious dentist meets a new patient. This patient is forty years old and has not been to a dentist except in emergency situations. What is the dentist's attitude? He knows that dentistry has spent nearly a century in educating people to come in every six months for preventive check-ups. It used to be that dentists only pulled teeth because the patient would wait until the tooth had decayed beyond saving. Do you think that this dentist does a root canal, saves the tooth, and then says to the patient to come back if his teeth ever hurt again? I should hope not!! You know that he schedules this patient into his office on a regular maintenance basis. You also may know many chiropractors who fix the pain and dismiss the patient. Why? I do not know. There must be some fundamental reason why these chiropractors do not want to be family practitioners and see patients on a preventive maintenance basis. We must get the patient started but then be willing to take them step by step into the Big Idea of Chiropractic. They need to bring their families and continue chiropractic care forever, just like you and your family do. The same is true on your spiritual journey. You must know that the world around you is not based on inward beauty and fulfillment. People are more concerned with what they wear and how they look than with any internal physical fitness or spiritual advance. One of the reasons for this is that the world is based on economics, and the inward journey is personal and not really marketable.

Avoid the negatives of the world. The bad news is for reactionary people. Give out positive thoughts to your patients and everyone around you. Start today by giving something spiritual to everyone. Start planting the seeds of a subluxation free, healthy body, free of pain and disease. Do this with each smile. Start practicing and teaching the necessity of adjustments, a pure bloodstream, and physical fitness. Help patients with their bad habits without judging or condemning. You can do this by thinking and speaking of the benefits of your regimen. Keep the patients focusing on the way they CAN become, not on how they are now.

Here is a theory of mine. Poverty, unhappiness, and disease are the results of negative thoughts which can lead to accidents, which lead to subluxations, which lead to symptoms and disease. I always try to make a mental picture of how I want the patients to be after they have followed my schedule and finished the correction with which I am striving to help them. Try to speak with authority, but always remember the first rule. The patient needs to know how much you care before they care how much you know. I feel that this is the most critical point, for when the caring begins to develop, you can create a lifetime patient. This is not controlling patients with your thinking mind. This is sealing the patient in with your purity of purpose and clinical skills. This is why you must be right in the office. You must be able to duplicate your service on each visit and then the patients always return. It is like honoring that early bond of faith, an unspoken understanding of the patients and their needs. When patients try to fill you with their negativity, do not take it personally or respond to their attitude. However, do quietly pray for them and go about adjusting and talking about the benefits which you know they can receive when all is corrected and their subluxations are stable. I have always had my prayers answered. I always see a calmness enter here, and the patient responds to my encouragement. Sometimes nothing is spoken at all after the adjustment, and somehow all is okay.

After more than twenty-five years in practice, I know what it is that keeps patients coming in for decades for regular adjustments. It is not the great genius of Tom Morgan. It is the duplication of the embrace written about above and the fact that I can clear them out and keep them this way. Their Innates heal their bodies, and they know somehow that the destructive processes, no matter how far progressed, have been reduced or changed into constructive regenerative processes. They also know that they are gaining on life. You see, medical doctors give no real faith in health. They give only treatments for symptomatic relief. Their system is based on sickness. The medical doctors must be respected for their sophisticated surgical techniques used in trauma cases as well as their dedication to monopolizing health care.

However, we chiropractors must always remember in politics that we have to remain a separate and distinct profession. We must work tirelessly to see that medicine does not duplicate our services. We must commit to biomechanics, particularly of the spine and to subluxation research and see that we do this TODAY. This is urgent!

If you are determined to get started on the chiropractic way of life, you need to get out of your old life. Take a period of time – three weeks – when you miss reading the newspaper or watching the news on television. Try to live only in your family and in your work. Take a twenty minute walk every day. There is something in rhythmatic exercise which tunes you inward. Walk briskly or jog. It is one of the very best exercises. I jog, and I find that it gives me much physical and spiritual satisfaction. The days on which you walk will be your best days, so walk every day!!!

RECEIVING THE POWER

"ONE CAN TRULY LEARN MORE FROM LIFE'S TRIALS
THAN FROM LIFE'S TRIUMPHS."
Unknown

When you have acceptance of yourself as a chiropractor, when you believe in your work and your mission, then you will know that you have some real purpose to your existence. This is an unthinking kind of faith which lets you accept everything without a negative. When you were a child, you believed everything completely. When you were shown a picture of an elephant, an animal which you had never seen, you asked about it. You were told, "It is an elephant," and you BELIEVED it was an elephant. This is child like faith, complete and innocent. Then you lost the faith – especially when someone laughed at what you were doing or saying or wearing. You began imperfection in thought, and worldly negatives grabbed you. Doubt, fear, hate, bigotry, envy – these are what the world has for you. Now, you must reprogram your brain not to accept this when you are trying to fulfill your purpose. I believe that all power comes from God – Innate – Life – Spirit – ALL. However, as a chiropractor, I also believe in saving faith – faith in Jesus Christ, salvation and eternal life. You can be so positive to achieve a volume practice, but your spiritual advance, your faith, your sanctification, your edification – these all belong to God. The "power" you receive comes from God and makes you great. What you have may make you famous, but what you are – a servant for Christ and His grace to you – is "receiving the power".

A chiropractor's success can be measured in the number of subluxations he or she corrects each day. How disciplined you are in your adjusting schedule and lectures and how many maintenance patients you have in your practice are all good gauges of this success. The next best gauge is the percentage of your gross income which is paid out for expenses.

A chiropractor told me when I was first out of college that I would be a large volume practitioner and far surpass his own large volume practice someday. He said that having a large volume practice was not hard, as long as you keep your fees reasonable and your service fast and efficient. What he wanted to relate was that the most difficult thing to do was to keep your act together. I did not really know what he meant then, because I was young and intent on learning everything I could about chiropractic. I know now that he was telling me about his inner life and the necessary disciplines – the suffering I would experience and the blessings from God and His saving grace that would make or break me by acceptance or rejection.

Today's society tries to mold everyone into the categories of success or failure. Most of these "types" are based on money. Chiropractors try to project the same illusion. If a chiropractor tried to explain his success to me, a seasoned practitioner, in terms of receipts, I would see only half the picture – money and practice. Management is vital, but your loving service shows what you are on the inside. Show me a chiropractor who guards his practice like a protective parent – show me a doctor who knows what peace and stress a volume practice can be and couple this with a doctor who examines himself and confesses his sins and prays to be delivered from them;

show me a doctor who knows who created him and where he should place all the real value in this life; show me a doctor who lives within his income, is free of debt and who has financially prepared for the years of physical decline; show me a doctor who always has a kind word for his fellow chiropractors, show me a chiropractor who gives back to his profession, church, and country; show me a doctor who works at growing spiritually when physical growth has changed; show me a doctor who resents the glitter of "things" of this world; show me a doctor who wants all his children to be chiropractors; show me this doctor, and I will show you a real success.

THE INVERTED PYRAMID

"IT IS NOT HOW MUCH TALENT YOU HAVE, BUT RATHER HOW WELL YOU USE WHAT LITTLE TALENT YOU HAVE."

Unknown

When you climb the pyramid of success to the top, and you reach the "point" from which you can perch and view the "lowlings" on the assent, you wonder about the youth of the pursuants. This is much like the great boxer who sees the young fighters challenging him for the championship and knows that time is certainly catching up with his reflexes. Then you must approach success as an inverted pyramid. By viewing your success in this way, you can level off at the top and not get stuck on the "point." The way you level off largely depends on your preparation.

On your way up the ladder of success, you have to plan for your destination and be prepared for the trappings of success – money, fame and other illusions. You have to utilize the trappings of the climb. You must invest wisely. Rule No. 1 is "Do not invest in something about which you know nothing." Putting faith in brokers, real estate wizards, and get rich quick investors has never worked for me. You also must try to keep your body in good physical condition. You must not listen to accolades or take them seriously. You must continue your education and study of chiropractic. You must know that it is what you do that counts, not what people say or write about you. You must know when to rest and when to work. I looked around me at a recent Whitehall seminar and saw the looks on the faces of many young doctors. I knew they had leased their Mercedes and their lean profit percentage of their actual net income was causing their youth to say, "It's okay to be deep in debt, I'm young, I can pay it off and then save my money later." It would have done little good to share with them my feelings that they need to be out of debt and holding a million dollars in tax free bonds. This is a real goal and one I know will take the financial stress off your back. I believe that without doing this, you are teetering on the tip of your pyramid, and the stress can cause you to die young, or die deep in debt. The high stress of being a doctor eventually comes down to your earning power or your saving power. Take it from a twenty-five year veteran and do what the Whitehall Management course tells you to do.

DON'T WALK, RUN

"SUCCESS IS RESOLUTION THAT IS NOT AFRAID OF SACRIFICE."

Unknown

Most of you reading this have listened to many teachers, learned all the skills and thought all the thoughts that you need to achieve great success. The rest is up to the ones who are willing to get started. B.J. aptly said, "Success consists in the climb."

The great and talented artist knows that he can never paint again unless he really chooses to do so. He can spend his days seeking pleasures. However, I have read where great artists and writers say that they have no choice. They are so obsessed with their talent that they have to dedicate all their lives to it. Shakespeare was around forty years old when he told someone that he thought he had written enough. He never wrote another page, and he died a few years later. I have seen chiropractors with great skill and patient management talents, but some were unwilling to put in the office hours necessary to achieve success commensurate with their abilities. People must decide whether to use their talents. Somewhere in their thoughts, they have to decide what goal they really want to achieve. Then they never look back but push on to completion. Today is the only day in which you can make a difference in this world. If you live in a daydream of rationalization, rejection, and negativity, then you will give back to God just that. Then the blessings will be few also.

But if you live in the world today as a striving, serving, giving individual, then you leave a little of the Master's love in all that you touch, and the world is improved.

The law of expression is dependent on the work which you do each day. The aim and attitude of your work allows this law to turn you into a great success. Expression must take place with each patient, each visit, each subluxation which you correct, today and FOREVER.

To achieve a volume practice, you must "see" it before you. You must "see" a parking lot full of cars and your waiting room full to overflowing. You must have the long office hours planned and a staff trained and dedicated to seeing large numbers of patients. You must begin the climb, and RUN – don't walk.

RIGHT THINKING

"WRONG THOUGHT PRODUCES WRONG ACTION WHICH PRODUCES ACCIDENTS WHICH PRODUCES SUBLUXATIONS, WHICH PRODUCE DISEASE."

A big problem that will hold you back is that most people reflect the opinions of others, not their own. That is why we, as chiropractors, cannot talk or think about what our patients talk and think about unless they come from a chiropractic background. We must have a mind fix on what we are doing and what we want for our patients. We do not "treat" our patients' minds like a psychologist does, nor do we try to talk them into or out of anything. We ADJUST. Have you ever noticed how much differently the patient acts after an adjustment, once he can finally understand what you are doing for him? I make it a habit never to say much about the Big Idea of chiropractic on the first couple of visits. I wait until the patient starts to "clear out." Then I begin to subject my influence toward what he needs to know about chiropractic, and how it relates to him. Then I have him come to my health class, and that is where I tell him everything I want him to know about chiropractic. I also believe that the patient does not learn everything I try to teach him, but one of the greatest benefits of the new patient health class is the doctor gets back to his basic reasons behind what he does and why he is a chiropractor. Make up your mind to "light one candle" in every patient through your patient lectures.

ABUNDANT PRACTICE

"THE IMPORTANT THING IS TO BE ABLE AT ANY MOMENT TO SACRIFICE WHAT WE ARE, FOR WHAT WE COULD BECOME."
Charles DuBois

Many people will tell you to slow down, to not ask for more, and to show moderation. I say, though, if it is right and natural, then go for it with all you have – flat out – one hundred percent effort.

There is abundance in the environment around us. The seed planted yields one thousand fold. Everything will produce to overabundance. Natural laws, and aging, however, check growth cycles and man has made many species become unnaturally extinct. Grab the concept of abundance and use it in your practice. The law of abundance is a natural phenomenon. You can have abundance in new patients. On life's journey, it is usually not how extreme you get that holds you back, but it is how timid you are. I believe that you must see abundance in your life, in your practice, in your family, in your bank account, and in your possessions. However, you must see abundance most of all in reproducing your efforts. The mark of a great teacher is in the fact that his students still remember his concepts, apply them, teach them to others and thank him later for his service to them. The same goes for being a great doctor. So serve out of your abundance. I always have and have never been sorry. I always feel rewarded by God for an honest effort with my patients. I never give up on a case. I always believe that Innate can help them to some extent. I keep working on my adjusting technique every day, every year. I want our research to show us how to serve more abundantly with even greater results. You see, I appreciate abundance!

FAITH IN YOURSELF

*"THERE ARE NO RED ROSES WITHOUT THORNS, NOR
VICTORIES WITHOUT BATTLES."*
Unknown

Never lose faith in yourself or your abilities. When you have
made mistakes, and things have not gone right, try not to get
"down" on yourself. This is a time to regroup and go deeper
within your spiritual life for the power of resolve. You have
to talk over your mistakes with God. Then you have to look
at your positive talents and know that you can do certain things
better or as well as anyone else that you know. Learn how to
use the secret of desire. When you get "down" on yourself,
there is more that goes astray than your self-esteem and self-
worth. You tend to believe the response your consciousness
makes to the world (negative). This alone detunes you. Then
you lose your desire and become a victim to the ways of the
world. I believe one of our greatest sins is being lazy. In
Scott Peck's book "A Road Less Traveled," there is a great
chapter on laziness. It explains how our talents, abilities, and
spiritual advances are greatly hindered by our own laziness.

Create a positive practice, one which is based on sound management principles as well as patient needs. You will begin
and end each day with momentum. A faith and confidence
momentum routine is somewhat boring, but be very disciplined
and very predictable. Then you create a positive schedule –
never late, never really behind, never tired, never symptomatic. You must, however, use discipline.

If you are an undisciplined practitioner, then you tend to lose your desire to help sick people get well. Then you lose yourself in hobbies or other pleasures instead. This leads to an undirected life and pretty soon, you also lose contact with what you were meant to achieve as well as the people whom you were supposed to serve. You turn to selfish intents and pursuits and begin to stick your thumb in your mouth every time things do not go your way. Instead of attacking weaknesses in your practice, you begin to complain and blame others for them. So look for the symptoms of selfishness. They can enslave you.

You have your own power. I believe that God always directs me to take a step. If it is right, it works out. If not, then maybe I forced things to happen to please me. Omniscient strength comes only from God. In "Newsweek" during the 1976 bicentennial celebration, there were interviews with immigrants who settled here. One such person was a one hundred year old man who was still selling newspapers in New York City. When asked about his life since coming to this country, he bragged on the freedom of American and said that here he could know his own power, have faith in his abilities, and accomplish whatever this knowledge brought. He had peace and happiness showing on his face. The blushes of your smile reveal a lot about your desire to use your power. The big secret of using desire is to feel right about what you want. Then you set your course for achieving your desires. YOU must begin – do not just talk about beginning. Use action. When you really feel your desire, circumstances will change to meet the atmosphere for achievement. It is putting your mind on a task and tuning out the negativity of the world. You must live in your own reality.

You must get moving. In your community, you have to get out and tell people what you are and what hope you have for them. You create the need to be their chiropractor. It is up to you to adjust as many patients as you can each day. You have to become responsible for your area NOW. There is an extreme abundance of subluxated people who need you and chiropractic. Get to these people somehow. If you are too economical to have a large enough office and enough equipment and staff, then you will need to start where you are and save for the larger office. Plan for fulfilling the need that is there in your community. Think "abundance." Do more advertising. Have a once a month, FREE children's clinic on Saturday mornings. DO SOMETHING. Stay busy.

We practice abundance in our daily lives now, but some abundance is detrimental. For example, we tend to eat too abundantly! Some smoke or drink in excess. We can let our habits get us out of control. On the other hand, how about practicing until midnight? That would certainly seem extreme to some, but remember, everything grows abundantly if you take care of it and work at it. The grass in your yard grows better after a rain. Without the proper care, it can get up to your waist. You can eat until you weigh three hundred pounds. Innate only obeys natural laws.

The secret is to channel your goals and patterns of work and practice until you achieve great abundance in the areas in which you need to grow. We are all slaves to agreeing and acting on precedent. We tend to do what everyone else is doing, wear what everyone else is wearing, and even think what everyone else is thinking. We tend to believe with the majority whether the doctrines are true or not. Myth or fact, this subtlety is responsible for training our subconscious to think and act in a certain way. The problem here is that this one pattern is responsible for our habits which can hold us captive. We spend our lifetimes trying to overcome unwanted habits. That is the reasoning behind the affirmations and the exercises herein. You must hold your constructive thoughts in a lasting picture to overcome negative habits. As Innate creates our tissues in a perfect manner, so must we work on carrying out that which we know we must do.

ARE YOU POSITIVE?

"I'VE NEVER SEEN A SUCCESSFUL PERSON WHO CRITICIZES HIS COLLEAGUES."

When I was in my last year at Palmer, I became deeply interested in being positive. I did not have an unusually negative attitude about myself, except like everyone else in the world, I wanted to be thinner, better looking, sing better, be smarter, etc. You see, I think all of us have too much negative self-image. I read every book I could find on the subject. Every book was soooo positive! I could not stand it that they were so positive! I loved reading the success books and stories. I was fascinated with the realism involved when regular "ole" people became unbelievably successful. A theme of consistency ran through these stories. Almost everyone had failures. It seemed as though they used their defeats to be even stronger in their positive resolve.

Have you ever visited a negative chiropractor? Egads! Have we got some negative chiropractors! I suggest that you visit every chiropractor in your town until you feel that you have visited ENOUGH! Remember the negatives and positives. Remember their offices, character, and make notes of those who encouraged or discouraged you. You need to fight negativity like a chronic subluxation. If you find yourself becoming negative, try this exercise:

- Get up early every morning and get to the office one hour earlier than usual.

- Write down at least three positive things that you did or plan to do that day. Make these "praises" or little pats on the back. They can be short, like replacing a burned out light bulb, or longer, like figuring out a new technique. Do this exercise every day for four months. What will happen is that you will begin to be assertive in a positive way. Something happens inside that seems to sort out negative and positive. You then decide where to live – in the positive, of course!
- The next time a chiropractor visits you or you visit one of them, tell them several positive things about themselves and their practice. If it is a new chiropractor, go out of your way to tell all the positive points of your community and chiropractic.
- The next time a patient wants to gossip about another doctor or say something detrimental about someone else, you need to offer two positives about that person, even if all you have positive to say is that he is one of God's children. As you bring out the positives, you assert this power into the patient and soon they will keep the negatives for someone else to hear.

I know a chiropractor who spends a lot of time running errands for his wife and children. He does this even to the point of interfering with his practice hours. This can be the first symptom that he is non-assertive or negative. He is also out of balance and this disrupts the balance in his family. To keep from becoming negative and non-assertive, practice the above exercises. Get your priorities straight, and make sure that your family understands where the emphasis is to be. They are not neglected, only in order.

The chiropractor must realize that it makes him negative to be away from his work. There is something very stabilizing about caring for many patients each day. You will not know this until you take a sabbatical for a year or two. I learned that it is a privilege to be a doctor and to have patients who need you. It is my destiny. On your days off, family must and should come first. You must have this free time to recharge your generator. Do this with the disciplines of the senses mentioned in a previous chapter. The worst part about being negative is the self-critical thoughts. When you make such a thought or statement concerning yourself, you create a totally detrimental living environment. Then you run the risk of becoming bogged down in your own self-pity. The key here is to detonate self-critical thoughts the instant they appear. NEVER fail to do this most important exercise. Remember, if you let the camel put his nose in your tent, pretty soon the entire camel is inside! DETONATE NEGATIVES, AS SOON AS THEY APPEAR, outside yourself and inside, too.

BE POSITIVE

"WHETHER YOU THINK IT'S HARD OR WHETHER YOU THINK IT'S EASY, YOU'RE RIGHT!"
Norman Vincent Peale

There is an old ally of doctors that has been used for centuries – the positive reinforcement of improvement. What doctor can resist taking credit for healing a patient and also taking some credit for fixing the malady? When a patient looks and moves better, can you resist bragging on them? As a chiropractor, I spend most of my day looking for positive clinical results, but then some doctors go home and function in society in a dolorous negative attitude. We will look at the way I have used a positive attitude to stay "up."

First, you have to know how to edit out all the patients' negatives. There is nothing so negatizing as physical illness. No one wants it, and no one can function mentally with a painful and symptomatic physical system. However, I hardly ever sympathize with the patient or repeat how sick he is with him. I let my staff do that while they are taking the patient information. The key to turning the patient's negativity to positivity is to only ask positive questions about his symptoms. At first I do not tell the patient that I can do anything about changing the symptoms or healing him; that the real healing power comes from his own Innate. I save that for later. My attitude is one of "quiet empathy" with a big, open, loving accepting heart. I do not care how he smells, looks, how much money he has, or how beastly his kids are acting.

NOTHING distracts my completely open and loving attitude on those first visits. I edit out all the "goat feathers" in life. I only ask questions about the symptoms that may help me locate and correct his subluxations, and then I motion him on the adjusting table for the initial examination. Next, as the patient is going down on the table, I begin talking to him about what I am going to do. This is positive talk. For instance, I might say "Fred (I always use first names, unless the patient is over eighty-five years old), I am going to conduct the preliminary examination now. We are going to check all your spinal balances and test your nerves, muscles, and joints for the cause of your problems." I continue on and on, talking constantly about what I am doing. I find the subluxations and tell him what is causing his problems. I ask God to help me correct these subluxations.

I was taught by Dr. Donald Pharoah at Palmer that a really good chiropractor could tell the patients' symptoms by motion and static palpation. Since college, I have correlated my palpation findings to the exact malposition of the vertebrae with particular emphasis on the A-P curves. When I located my first subluxation and its symptoms at Palmer, I began programming my cortical software to look for a subluxation and to remember just how it palpated. I could then recognize the same subluxation/symptoms when I came across them again. I developed this "touch and tell" system to the point where I would scan each patient on every visit for symptoms other than what was listed and tell him the cause. This system is so successful that nearly all of my patients expect me to tell them how they are doing rather than them repeating their symptoms to me or telling me how they "feel." By correlating the subluxation as the cause of their symptoms, I believe I can break down the medical indoctrination in their brains, and they soon start to think like chiropractors (i.e. - causes and correction instead of symptoms and treatment). They then begin to look to the spine for health. These positive actions cause practice to be fun, and this can only come from years of training patients to the spine, the adjustment, and the importance of regular check-ups. Asymptomatic patients and their families presenting on regular schedules are the bedrock and the mainstays of a positive, happy practice. If you are merely trying to help the patient's symptoms with the adjustment or if you are only interested in decreasing the patient's pain, then you are really practicing like a medical doctor. This is also why the medical doctors' offices usually seem depressing, negative and over decorated. The key is to keep our minds focused on the "cause" and how to help Innate begin to heal the patient by correcting the subluxations.

THE WORLD'S INFLUENCE

"PATIENTS DO NOT CARE HOW MUCH YOU KNOW UNTIL THEY KNOW HOW MUCH YOU CARE."

When you read the newspaper, edit out the negatives. Do not let them in! On television do not watch the negative, violent programs. Instead watch something real and entertaining. Edit your contact with people outside also. When your pastor asks everyone to pray for the doctors and medicine to cure people, replace those words in your mind with "Pray for more chiropractors, giving more adjustments, releasing God's power of healing, and teaching more people about internal physical fitness and chiropractic." Replace every negative you can with your own positive. Remember, chiropractic builds natural immunity. This is not just related to invasive organisms but also to invasive and negative attitudes and effects. Become immune to negative things, news, and gossip – especially about other chiropractors! In battle every corps carries its color guard (flag) to remind it of previous battles and of what is expected from it. Likewise, we are at war with a pseudo-health pro-sickness assumption of medicine.

It is up to you to bring light to the patients, as well as to the decades of fear which have been fed into their brains that when they are symptomatic they are out of control or next to death and that they need a medical doctor or a pill to change them from the outside. The eradication of this false assumption is the primary objective of a chiropractor. We can do it with adjustments and teaching.

BELIEF SYSTEMS

"ONE WHO IS BORN IN THE FIRE WILL NOT WILT IN THE SUN."
Old Korean Proverb

What do you really believe? Do you believe if it is raining that it is going to be a "bad" day? If you do, get busy studying your beliefs and creating some counter-beliefs to dissipate this terrible problem. Some beliefs are inherited from family members. Remember your mom saying, "If you keep eating so much, you will be fat," or "If you do not study, you will fail," or "If you do not wear a coat, you will catch cold." We do not say things like that do we? Nooo, not much!! I will give you a project. Each day for the next two months, get up in the morning and say three positive things to each of your children and to your wife. For instance, "You look nice this morning," "You smell sweet," "You sure look pretty," or even "Have a good day." The most important thing to build positive images is to say "I love you" every morning and every night – the most receptive times. Have your staff come in early each morning and tell you three positive things about you, your practice, your person, anything. Then you tell them three positives, such as "You look nice," etc. Then stand back and watch what happens! You do this to your patients, and now you can do it for your family and your staff. Make these positives as real and as accurate as possible. Finally, it is probably most important what you say and think about yourself. Believe and see to it that you are subluxation – free, healthy, physically in shape, as organically nourished as possible, positive, and happy to serve sick people, release life, and teach about health and its origin. You are saving some money and providing spiritual and material support for your family and friends. You are adding contributions to chiropractic research, your college, church, family, and friends, and it is returning one thousand fold.

After you say three positive things to your staff and family, give a couple of commands with the words "I want you to ... smile bigger than ever to each patient, be on time, talk more about subluxations and causes to the patients, give them more confidence that Innate can heal them, cut the grass, study with a purpose, etc." Then see what happens. Just the positivity will cause love and enthusiasm to ensue. The big release here and your positive work will cause you to "come out of yourself," giving more to those with whom you live and work. HAVE FUN!

I have always been too serious. I am happy, but I do not go out of my way to have fun. I think the key here is to be both serious and funny.

WHAT DO YOU HAVE TO GIVE?

A DOCTOR NEVER MAKES THE STATEMENT: "I WISH I HAD SPENT MORE TIME IN THE OFFICE AND LESS TIME WITH MY FAMILY."

When I first began practice, I would concentrate on the fact that I was just out of college, had learned all the latest techniques and had the newest, most modern equipment. I would ride down the street and draw a big imaginary marker through medical and other chiropractic offices. I felt sure that everyone would see that I was the only one around who was there to help. When I opened my last office in Georgia, I had twenty years of experience behind me, and my thoughts were constantly on the fact that I had this experience. I visualized myself as the authority on difficult and unusual cases. I had many come in for second opinions and soon established my reputation as an expert doctor. I had four other chiropractors on the same street so I immediately erased them from view. My goal was simple. I wanted to offer my very experienced skills at a reasonable fee in order to build up a large volume practice.

People had to try me to find out what I could do. I created this dome or vacuum over my office and drew a mental picture of many patients coming into this dome. I had one hundred patients the first month and hit fifty visits in one day during the second month.

The key here is not to let anything make you negative. If there are weaknesses in management, procedure, technique, then go get help! Work, study, and never slow down learning the success tools.

If I had any great regret in my years of practice, it was that I was overcommitted to my practice. Office hours from 8:00 A.M. to 9:00 P.M. do not leave much time to spend with the family. I recommend that you start out this way, but make sure that you also make time for the important people in your life – your wife, children, other family members, and friends. I am sure that every father who has worked like I have looks back and wonders what the kids remember about growing up with Dad. They may think, "I know I could have done better so that you would pay attention to me." Try to work in a routine schedule of activities with each child and a special date with your wife each week. Don't forget now – it takes more than trying.

MONEY

"IF YOU ARE NOT GRATEFUL WITH A MEAGER INCOME, YOU WILL NEVER BE GRATEFUL WITH ABUNDANCE."
T. O. Morgan, B.S., D.C.

You like money? I do. It is friendly, warm, and green – my favorite color. It matches all the clothes in my wardrobe. You need to like it. What happens in computer language when you put in information about the weather? You get out information about the weather! If you put in junk, you get out junk! Put money thoughts into your cortical computer. Do not be shy. Put in BIG BUCKS! Money, money, money, NICE!

In the Bible, Jesus talked more about wealth than about any other subject. He advocated the need for everyone to have riches, but there was a golden thread woven through these parables. It is called spiritual wealth. The green stuff will not buy it, and new cars, homes, planes, and boats will not bring you any closer to it either. Wives, children, lovers, family, friends, practice, anything outside yourself will not bring it either. Nope. You must see Flip Wilson's analogy, "What you see (in your heart) is what you get!" If you do not pray, meditate, read spiritual books regularly, examine your sins, explore the real intent of your heart; if you do not pray to God for a strong will to overcome your weaknesses, if you do not do these every day and every way, then you cannot know spiritual wealth, and the wage for that sin is death (spiritual death). That is the worst kind.

I bought three or four Cadillacs. If I gave them just a tad amount of power over spirit, what would happen? Sure enough, someone would scratch them or dent them or the gas gauge would quit working! That is when I would get another one! I bought Corvettes, and the cops followed me around with green stamps. Now I buy diesel Mercedes' and I cannot catch up with the cops! I even bought a fast airplane, and it soon got REAL important. Of course, I was a grand and glorious pilot in my own mind. That is when I tried to beat a thunderstorm into an airport and forgot to put down the landing gear. It was REAL hard to get Mary Ann and the kids to ride with such a glorious pilot after that! I bought Tennessee Walking horses by the trailer load. I had enough horses to keep each leg up, twenty-four hours a day. I even got the gang to shovel horse manure on a regular basis until I burned them out. I built the largest home in my town. It had an indoor heated swimming pool so we could swim in the winter. Man, if material things could get through with purpose, it would have done this for me. You might think it would be nice. However, if your spiritual life is progressing, and you only think kindly of your material possessions they do not have power over you. When you count your blessings each day, do not leave out the material but ALWAYS start with the spiritual. Beg for mercy (not getting what you deserve) and accept grace (a blessing unearned) with humble thanks.

I over-extended myself for over a decade by obtaining a high political office. After getting three governors to appoint me to three five year terms on the Mississippi Board of Chiropractic Examiners and after being elected four times to high I.C.A. positions, as well as keeping up my positions on the Life Foundation and Life College Boards, I found that this mostly took me away from my family more and more. Although my ego was much massaged, there was an ultimate satisfaction to be gained from serving. The point is BALANCE – ninety-eight percent spiritual life and two percent material life. That is where your heart has to be, just HAS to be.

The key here is like believing your parents when you were a teenager. I remember thinking, "You cannot believe those old folks. They are out of date." You must know yourself. So set all the money goals, and get that money. You need it and deserve it so GET it. Then you will see. Remember, you can accumulate material and spiritual wealth at the same time. Think about it!

HAPPINESS IS FELT IN THE PROCESS

*"HAPPINESS COMES FROM SOMETHING YOU DO.
JOY COMES FROM SOMETHING DONE FOR YOU."*
(e.g. the gift of the cross)
Gene Cunningham

Reaching for your goals and traveling the spiritual highway brings real happiness. Many people believe that they would be happy IF they "just had an office like yours." When you think of the happiness derived from your office, though, you know that it was in its conception, planning, building, selecting what it was to be, how it was to look, and yes, the work it took to achieve those goals. That brings happiness. The happiness you feel inside is there during the process. Once it is all done you are thankful, but you must then think another thought, plan another plan, keep on keeping on! Be happy in your practice today. Do not let what you would like to happen tomorrow spoil what happiness there is for you now. Keep a new thought, or technique, equipment, improvements – something – in mind always for your practice. Look for these things. Be thankful for them when they are achieved and make this process called living your "best thing." True God-centered, inner directed, intensive desires are almost unstoppable. They must be held in your mind in such a secret, protective recess that this fix cannot be unlocked except by achievement. Some say that this is self-concentration, but it is more than that. These real desires must be couched deep within the secret recesses of your mind and are so accentuated by your consciousness that they are a reality even before anyone can see them happen. Anyone who has reaped success has felt the magic of a one-track mind, bent on intensive desire to achieve the success with his own power. Now is the time to stop believing that some people are just lucky. If you are courageous, then believe that the laws of success can work for you. Give thanks to God, and take on a new air of free adventure and happiness in life. Look at each day for signs predicting what you are holding within as truth forthcoming. Get yourself out of a rut. Show God your courage and determination.

If it is money that you most desire, then you must find out where it can originate. What you really want is to give more service. Oh, sure, there is a million dollar lottery in your state, but God prefers that you appreciate money, and service is the only real way to appreciate where and how you receive such wealth. Raising fees never made anyone really wealthy. You must also increase your volume. There must be more patients. These must be properly managed. You must collect your fee. You must feel that you are giving an invaluable service.

CONTROL OF YOURSELF

"FOR EVERY GOOD YOU ACCOMPLISH, THERE IS SOMEONE WHO WILL TELL YOU IT CAN'T BE DONE."
Ralph Waldo Emerson

You are trained in chiropractic college how to be a doctor. One of the ways a doctor must condition himself is to become calm in acute situations. The pain and excitement in the patient or condition mandates that the doctor be as calm as possible because he has to think and make decisions. I know chiropractors who are like Dr. Jekyll and Mr. Hyde in and out of their offices. They have complete professional manners while dealing with their patients, but outside the office, they are subject to habits of anger, jealousy, fear, worry, and other habits that often bring disaster. A successful doctor with a large practice may be in his third marriage, atheistic, addicted to chemicals, grossly overweight, and/or overbearing with his children, wife, friends and pets. Every destructive emotion is a wasteful emotion that wastes your energy and makes you less able to face daily living. One of the best ways that I deal with negative emotions is to exercise.

When I run, I feel myself leave the part of Tom Morgan that I do not care for behind in the dust. It is not that I am a great jogger, but there is some cerebral change when you increase oxygen supply, and the vascular dilation that occurs clears out the tubes and starts your brain over clean again. What I think it really does is to balance your chemistry, once the negative emotions have clearly unbalanced it. You cannot crush all your negative emotions, but you can start with a point-counterpoint to make something out of your negative thoughts and turn them into positives. Find the point which turns you around into love, happiness, and contentment. You must first resolve to change. Anyone who has broken a bad habit can tell you that there are a lot of tricks to try to fool yourself, but when it comes down to the bottom line, it takes a willful resolve to commit to a decision and then you wait for God's grace. You must be prepared and have a willingness to know that you will probably fail many times, but ultimately, you will change. I have found that people who change their attitudes about their habits, expose themselves, and by using the laws which we have discussed, also lost their need for liquor, drugs, gluttony, and other habits which enslave humanity.

THE LAW OF LIMITATION

"MANY MEN DESIRE TO BECOME GODS, BUT ONLY ONE GOD DESIRED TO BECOME MAN."
Unknown

What are your limitations? Are they bound by physical and mental capabilities? This is true only to an extent. In fantasy and fiction, there is no law of limitation. In matter, there are physical limitations. What we want to look at is the fact that limits you set for yourself, are bound by spiritual and physical laws, but there is no limit to your dreams and desires. The limit is your actions. More important is your willingness to see it through – to work at it day and night – even with defeat or under duress. You need to put yourself into a position where God can use you, and He will put you in a position that defies all imagination. That is what one thousand, two hundred visits per week is all about. That is the position I was in. That was a point of time in my life that may be unimaginable to most chiropractors, but nevertheless, it was my position. As I look back, I realize that it was also my destiny, that God picked this for me to do. What is difficult is to not take yourself and your accomplishments too seriously, not to make your supreme self the master, not to believe the Devil's lie that you can create all things, and that you are God. If this occurs, your pride in your weak self puffs up and pretty soon, you are too "good" to care for Mr. Average Patient. Lastly, you must live for tomorrow, using the past as a springboard to urge you on, not for placation or passivity.

PUNISHMENT OR REWARD

*"REPUTATION IS WHAT OTHERS THINK YOU ARE;
CHARACTER IS WHAT GOD KNOWS YOU ARE."*
Unknown

There is no law of punishment or reward. There is only harmony with natural laws or disharmony. You choose which it will be. Just as a vertebral subluxation causes disharmony of function, so disharmonious thoughts and actions cause negative emotions, poverty, fear, and doubt. It is time to sublimate your consciousness and make positive commitments. Then decide with all your conscious power to act out these positive thoughts. There is less to fear from outside competition than from inside inefficiency, lack of courtesy, and carelessness. Discipline is the key here, and the secret is to start today and continue no matter what. When you reach that zone, try to understand that it is not you who "doeth the work, but the Father within."

DIVINE VIEWPOINT

"TO EACH IS GIVEN A BOOK OF RULES, A SHAPELESS MASS, A BAG OF TOOLS... AND EACH MAY MAKE 'ERE LIFE HAS FLOWN, A STUMBLING BLOCK, OR A STEP-PING STONE."
Delta Sigma Chi Rule Book

Moses was an overwhelmingly beautiful child. He later became a most handsome man. He was more intelligent than most people of his time. He could have become the pharaoh of Egypt, since he had been raised as the son of one of pharaoh's daughters. He was offered every worldly thing which his ancient civilization had to offer. However, he chose a different path than fortune and fame. Why? He chose not present pleasures, but eternity with God (Heb. 3:5). God let Moses see the future. He chose forty years in the desert with two and one half million Jews, and eternity with God.

My teenage idol, Elvis Presley, seemingly had everything. He had all the money and things he could buy. He had the ability to fulfill any lust with whomever he chose. He had enormous power and talent. He fulfilled his purpose in music. Why is it that many celebrities cannot see the future and choose the path of destruction, instead of eternity with God? One answer could be that they choose to solve human problems with human solutions, instead of with divine ones.

Human viewpoint versus divine viewpoint shows that one is good for the short term, while the other is good for eternity.

How do you decide? Sit down and think of someone you know personally, or whose work you have studied, who has given all they have in talent, energy and resources to achieve something for others. You will soon turn up one primary reason for your decision to become a chiropractor – you are to help others.

I believe that this is why chiropractic is truly a God inspired science. This is why we must keep it drugless, and based on the innate recuperative powers of the body. B.J. Palmer lectured on "slipping and checking." He said you are always doing one or the other. You are either growing or moving backwards. It takes constant self discipline and examination to search out the enemy which would have you change your standard.

Nearly everyone has heard of General William Booth, the founder of the Salvation Army. He was tall, gangly, Lincolnesque figure who worked in a pawn shop and preached part time. One day, as he passed a gin brothel, he felt a stirring within him which changed the world. He had thought that he wanted to be a missionary, but as he saw the people who frequented such places as the brothel, he wondered where he could go and find such heathens as these, or where else the labor for God would be so great. He then set out to serve these forgotten people better than anyone else. He did this twenty-four hours a day, seven days a week. William left footprints in stone, and the Salvation Army will carry on his work. In less than twenty-five years, the Salvation Army grew to one hundred and two thousand, nine hundred centers. Almost fifty million dollars had been raised for the under-privileged and Salvation Army officers were holding over fifty thousand meetings each week. If you do only for your-self, your footprints will be made in sand and will disappear when you leave this earth. Dedicate some of yourself to leaving something good here after you are gone. Live for others. Unselfish service is an uncommon occurrence. Because you work for yourself, you can give more than you take. Make this a spiritual goal for yourself.

A key here is to protect yourself from damage to your spiritual armor. You do this by not taking any prisoners. The prisoners are caused by depending on someone or something to do for you what only God can do. It is also caused by criticizing, gossiping, hating, envying, being jealous, letting anger rule you, and being self-centered. Let us try in our working hours to lose ourselves in service. If we do this, I believe that we all can experience the dedication felt by William Booth.

DISCIPLINE – THE KEY TO SUCCESS

"ENTHUSIASM AND EMOTIONALISM HAVE A DEFINITE PLACE – TO MAKE THESE A REALITY, YOU MUST CONNECT THEM TO YOUR GOALS."

When my kids were in their teens, and staying on the phone incessantly, I would sometimes hear them talking with friends about what they like, or more aptly, about what they did not like, who was stuck up, and on and on. You see, growing up must be a process of trial and error. You accept some things, and question others, but you mostly have to fall down before you can get up. I am always glad though, to see a child who respects the parents, and parents who care enough to discipline their child. That way, when the parents are gone, the child will not be so rebellious as to be unable to turn to respect God.

We adults must not do childish things nor should we be captive to childish habits. There are always things that teenagers do not like about themselves, and it is hard for them to appreciate what God has made. You must love yourself. Somehow you must do something each day that shows you that you love your spirit and your flesh. If you overeat, overdrink, oversmoke, under exercise, watch negative TV shows, and do not seek spiritual advance, can you love yourself each day? The secret is discipline. Doing daily disciplines feed back positive data. Your discipline must encompass three areas – physical, mental, and spiritual. What we have been talking about throughout this book is the fact that you have natural laws available to work with each day, and your discipline helps keep you on course. People are attracted to one who is right on the inside. Your ability to help people will increase and you will find yourself in leadership positions and receiving accolades for things that will seem routine for you. Remember to take these two manmade impostors – honor and glory – for what they are worth! But always be thankful that you could have sublimated yourself and disciplined yourself to such a degree that recognition was forthcoming. NOW – GO ON SERVING!

DECISION TIME

"IF YOU KEEP POSTPONING A DECISION, YOUR INDECISION BECOMES YOUR ONLY DECISION."

There are many times in our lives when we are not free to function as we would like. We know that we are divided over problems and decisions which we continually put off making. We are only functioning at half speed, doing the same things without freedom. We are held back by our own indecision. The way to become free on the inside where we can function properly is to commit. This same concept relates to health and our chiropractic patients. For example, some people do not really want to commit to health. In fact, some people seem to enjoy being disabled and pampered over their symptoms. One of the most important facets of success in practice involves being able to identify these people and to change their perspectives on health care. It is so important to get patients to actually commit to chiropractic care on the first few visits. As a chiropractor, you should make sure that you explain all their X-rays and examination findings with the utmost care and precision. Then you need to explain to them about the Big Idea behind chiropractic. The average case should commit to visiting you for at least the first fifteen adjustments. It is your job, during that time, to draw a larger commitment from them regarding their health.

Ideally, they should fully understand about the importance of chiropractic care and be ready to continue adjustments for the rest of their lives. If they do not make this commitment, they will not make lasting chiropractic patients. If they are on the verge of committing, it is important for you as the chiropractor to find out what is keeping them from making the ultimate decision. For example, is it finances? Misunderstanding? Other things? You need to be able to determine whether they really want to get well.

The chiropractor also needs to make a commitment to his practice and then stick to it. Only then are you free to move into that zone of success where peace and understanding reside. The happiness and completeness you receive each day comes from doing your very best for as many people as possible. Sometimes decisions are painful either way you go. It is painful to tell a patient to find another chiropractor if he cannot commit to coming to you for the needed adjustments, but sometimes that is the only answer. So you need to make your office policies and then STICK TO THEM! Believe me, if the indecision drags on, it only increases inefficiency and creates negativity in your mind.

BONDING

"CAN YOU HAVE AN INNATE-TO-INNATE BOND WITH YOUR PATIENTS? I THINK SO!"

It is important here to try to explain how chiropractic practices are built and maintained. First and most common is the austere, professional, white-coat approach. The doctor is learned and obviously skilled in methods and procedures not studied or understood by the patient. The doctor completes the history and physical examinations and then begins to hypothesize for possible diagnosis and care. On one hand is the medical approach to diagnosis – diagnosis by exclusion which requires a battery of tests, mostly to protect the doctor for malpractice purposes. If the doctor really likes his work and likes people, then he develops a "head" bond with the patient. The patient is awed by the doctor's intelligence, wit, or other bonding traits. I believe that political medicine wants the patient to be trained to feel a need to put faith in someone or some treatment to eradicate his symptoms. I knew of a neurosurgeon in the city where I practiced who constantly cursed at his patients! He seemed angry at everyone and everything. When I would ask my patients why they continued care and even submitted to surgery occasionally, not to mention the oral abuse which he always gave them, they would remark, "He was highly recommended" or "He said I had to have surgery right now in order to get well." I have not had a great deal of contact with medical doctors, but the ones I have talked with on a personal level always make fun of the "dumb" patients and indicate it to be a great chore and service even to see them. In the Army, when I was a medical corpsman, I was befriended by a medical doctor who had just finished his residency. He was very interested in explaining to the soldiers what their conditions were related to and what pills they should not take. The troops were clearly not interested, and most of the time, they thought he was crazy or bizarre in his approach because they definitely knew that pills were indeed what they needed. I can see this same gentleman become a mute, multi-prescription, shotgun general practitioner just a few years after seeing how the people have been trained to sickness and pills. Hopefully, he went into psychiatry! What struck me about this highly trained man, though, was his smug supremacy attitude toward health care. Medical School had done a number on him. He was telling me about the new birth control pill, and how medicine was going to solve the world's reproduction and hunger problems. He said that the gynecologists were being taught to do hysterectomies at even the slightest sign of difficulty. He also said that first year medical students were writing the chambers of commerce in different cities to discover the money and prestige to be found in the profession. I was appalled by his lack of concern for the needs of the sick. During one of our long days at the army dispensary, I suggested an experiment. The medical doctor would take histories of ten men and write down present symptoms and past conditions. Then I would perform a static spinal examination and tell the medical doctor what symptoms I found. I was ninety per cent accurate on all present symptoms and chronic conditions. Since these were young men, there were not now many problems other than headaches, sinus, asthma, stomach complaints, and back and leg problems. However, the medical doctor was impressed.

The only time I make a truly "head" bond with a patient is when he has been a close contact OUTSIDE the office before becoming a patient. This might be a longtime friend, my horse trainer, or someone else. The reason for this difference is there is a need for a new contact when you are visiting a doctor for the first time. He is a doctor, not "ole Tom" with whom you grew up. Some people want to have this almost reverent contact with their doctor. I believe that this is not always wrong. However, the doctor should also be aware himself of the need to create a deep, sensitive, almost spiritual bond with the patient. This Innate bond must prevail if the patient's best interests are always to be paramount. Only with this true "love" bond can doctors resist the omnipresent human tendency to become unscrupulous and enamored with their power over people.

Many doctors are unhappy and can even become evil because of the power they feel they possess over their patients. The tendency to create a "head" bond with the patient must be averted, as you become "friendly" and learn of acquaintances whom both of you know. For example, the "head" bond will give you the urge to try to become "likeable." This, however, is not what you want. You want to love and to hone in on the health goal you have set for this patient.

To establish an Innate-to-Innate bond is the ultimate in the doctor-patient relationship. In order to do this, you must be in a mental state of selflessness as you go through your diagnostic routines. There has to be that earnest longing for the spiritual embrace with the patient, where you can speak and act with an authority which is not overbearing, but clearly concerned. This may sound unusual, but I would often stare at X-rays and busy myself with busywork to keep from facing a patient for the report, if I did not feel led to a particular point that was relative only to that person. I call this "receiving divine authority." When it would come, only then would I present the report in the adjusting room and go over the

X-rays and findings as well as tell the patient what I understood to be the particular problem and what I expected to accomplish. This starts the bonding process. To be able to do this with new patients, and more importantly, to feel this bond (it is such a peaceful feeling) on each visit, year after year, is the absolute "raison d'être" of being a chiropractor. It is a blessing beyond description. My hope in this book is for you to see what it takes to get in the position of love and service to multitudes of people who can benefit from chiropractic. I always felt that God sent my patients to me and that they were there because they needed an adjustment. When I first started practice, I instructed my chiropractic assistants to let me see everyone who comes through the front door. I see these people sitting in the adjusting rooms with their friends who are the patients, and as I sense the fear of the unknown from them, I begin to mount my search for a position that enables me to motion to them with a few words. They are suddenly going down on the adjusting table, and I am "reading" their spines and examining them. I have done this for more than twenty years and have not experienced any negativity. When the patient is brought up off the table, I explain the exam and the chiropractic charts. I then make recommendations for X-rays and adjustments, which are usually followed.

LOVE

*"I BELIEVE THAT WE ARE ALL CALLED TO AN INCES-
SANT OCCUPATION WITH GOD."*

I want to write more on the subject of love. There are many
kinds of love, and we are in the middle of a transition – our
own. We either choose to take the time to see people, listen
to people, love people, and be involved with people, or we
are alone, feeling sorry for ourselves and being possessed by
fear. I believe that it is impossible to attract large masses of
people without that inward message of "This I have to give."

There have been more than fifteen thousand individual patients
who have chosen to come to my office, to fill out the forms,
and "meet" the doctor. As for me, I have been there to serve.
I have tried to give all I had to each one. What did they give
me? They gave me their faith, their time, and their money. I
watched a documentary the other night about my teenage
idol, Elvis Presley. The last words on the show were spoken
by his good friend and fellow performer, Sammy Davis Jr.
Sammy said something to this effect: "Elvis gave his talent
and was only at his best when he was onstage. We took this
love he projected from the stage and believed it to be his
greatest talent. He gave us all he had. None of us can do
more, and what he did for us in this way was good. So, on
that basis, his life was right." That is the way we chiropractors must be. We must be at our best when we are serving
and loving those who we are fortunate enough to have visit
us. How many more could we serve if we could just lose our

thoughts about ourselves and begin to seek out the sick and infirm? How many more could we serve if we could integrate ourselves into the masses of minds needing the message of chiropractic and the benefit to be gained through the adjustment? How many people, right now, are thinking that they would see a chiropractor if only someone would let down the barriers and welcome them in unconditionally? You can help these people, but you must be willing to go to any lengths to make your services convenient, affordable, reasonable, and effective.

Right now, you may feel flooded with ideas for your practice. The only thing that ultimately holds us back is our laziness. We have to act, and we have to get started NOW.

We are as much responsible for creating love in this world, by giving adjustments, as anyone else is. We have a greater opportunity than most people to do this because we get to touch people. People need to be touched in order to feel really loved. On an average day in America, sixty-nine subluxated, lonely, sick people commit suicide. Every eight minutes, someone is raped; every twenty-seven minutes, someone is murdered. Someone is robbed every seventy-six seconds. Someone you know may be involved in this sickness, someone you can adjust, someone to whom you can give love. Start out with the children. Every day nine thousand and seventy-seven babies are born. Must they become victims of the medical chain of specialists who will inoculate them and train them to hate symptoms, viruses, fevers, and infections? Will someone please tell these parents the truth and serve their children? Also, what about the nursing homes? Just go take a peek at what medicine has created with its technology of keeping the systems counter functioning just to sustain what doctors call being "alive." The bedfast people in those places will follow you down the hall with their eyes. Who will tell them, as Leo Buscaglia says, "Age has nothing to do with being senile. Senility is just feeling that you have no more options left." We can offer chiropractic care as a viable option. It is desperately needed in this sick and suffering society. Someone must start seeking out the senior citizens and urging them to stay with their adjustments. Encourage your elderly patients to take an adjustment every week for the rest of their lives, just as you do with your parents. In your health lectures, tell the patients about the wonderful philosophy of chiropractic. Tell them about how the real doctor is within, and you want to help them find faith in Innate and its self-healing mechanism. Only with enough chiropractors adjusting, and only when pure bloodstreams become a moral obligation for each person, and only when sixty million Valium prescriptions are NOT given each year in America will our job be finished. We all know that it is ultimately up to us, not to anyone else. Listen to the words and the feeling behind the words written by Mr. Ziner on personal revelation.

"We must remind ourselves, however, that no change takes place without working hard and without getting your hands dirty. There are no formulae and no books to memorize on becoming. I only know this: I exist, I am, I am here, I am becoming, I make my life, and no one else makes it for me. I must face my own shortcomings, mistakes, transgressions. No one can suffer my non-being as I do, but tomorrow is another day, and I must decide to leave my bed and love again. And if I fail, I do not have the comfort of blaming you or life or God."

When you get up each day, try to look in the mirror and say to yourself, "The most important thing today is getting my attitude right and making myself the greatest, grandest, most loving person in the world." Say this because this is what you are giving to your patients, wife, children, friends, and life itself. Let your heart, not your procedures, or fees, direct your service to your patients. Your heart must say to each person, "The reason for your being here is for me to give you my services and my love." Let the front office handle the book work. I am so incensed with this thought that I try never to talk about fees or money with my patients. I have a standard answer to everyone who asks me about changing the way they pay. I say, "Just tell my wife at the desk. She takes care of all the financial work." The fact is, I don't listen to what they say, and I could not care less about their money problems. It detunes me to let this in so I edit it out of my life and I let Mary Ann work it out. I have to laugh because it took years for Mary Ann to figure out that if she did not make the patient hold up his end financially, I NEVER would. This was one of my major weaknesses, and I owe much to Dr. Bill Harris for helping me overcome this problem. We are now collecting more for our services than ever before. However, I never forget my free patients. I always have some regular free patients whom I cherish. God always repays me in blessings – more than tenfold. If you do not have a couple of regular free patients, then you know that you are not really giving all that you have.

IT IS NEVER TOO LATE

"I DON'T THINK MUCH OF A MAN WHO IS NOT WISER TODAY THAN HE WAS YESTERDAY."
A. Lincoln

I know a seventy-five-year-old chiropractor who is always buying new technique equipment. He seems to stay enthused about chiropractic and is committed to learning the latest techniques. He probably has practiced a hundred thousand hours. I also know a twenty-five-year-old chiropractor just starting out, who brags that he will only work three days a week and only accept paying patients. Every doctor is different, but I cannot help feeling that the old doctor has better days and enjoys life more fully. The advertising world wants to program everyone into the belief that youth is where real happiness occurs. It is hard to make wrinkles glamorous on television. It is also not the real world on television. It is never too late to make your dreams come true. You must first believe in yourself and your dreams and then act always as if they were true. Science says that our body's soft tissue is made over every eleven months. How many new yous have been created? You must never respond to the fact that you could do so much more when you were younger. What purpose does that serve? Take a lesson which I learned from an old bird-dog trainer. I went to his kennel one day, and he wanted me to see his finest dog. He showed me a liver and white setter who looked pretty old. He said, "This dog is seventeen years old." I asked him if that was not the end of a dog's lifespan. He remarked that it was – in fact, past the end, but old "Pat" did not know it. He said that when he took Pat hunting, the dog would get just as excited, maybe more so than the young dogs. When he did let Pat out of the truck, Pat would hunt just like he always did for the first ten minutes. That is the way it has got to be. It does not matter if you cannot hunt all day. It matters that you can still give one hundred percent of your very best, even if it is only for ten minutes.

I remember my first Palmer College Homecoming when they started recognizing the fifty-year practitioners. Some of these men and women would literally run up on the stage to get their awards. The key is not what your number says, but how you feel and what kind of power and faith your life and knowledge have brought you. No matter what, do not let anything, especially a negative thought, keep you from doing what you resolve to do. Saint Paul wrote the church members at Corinth to press on, run your race, the stands are full of supporters. The plea is not to quit and not to run off the track.

Make up your mind that there is no such thing as retirement for you. You may change where you live and what you are doing, but you must be involved in something that requires someone to depend on you. You have to have a reason to get up each day, and it must be based on someone else needing you, not on your own wants. This is a great way to stay out of yourself. Try to lose yourself in service each day. It is not coincidence that men die soon after they retire. Do not get caught in the trap. Keep on serving.

SYMPTOMS AND CONDITIONS

"AN ERROR NO WIDER THAN A HAIR WILL LEAD A HUNDRED MILES AWAY FROM GOD."

A chiropractor can never be caught symptomatic. He cannot ever miss a day in the office because of symptoms. You must always recognize symptoms and conditions for what they are. You deserve them if you let yourself get in the climate that produces them. In all your work and teachings, you must set an example to the world. You must be subluxation-free, in top physical condition, and consume pure food and water. A pure bloodstream and clear nervous system is no accident. It has to be part of your daily regimen. If you respond to your symptoms, it means that you want sympathy and that is for greeting cards! You must treat symptoms and conditions as a result of breaking natural laws. Just as you must keep your innermost desires a secret, so must you keep your symptoms secret and get the cause corrected so that you can stay productive. No one is more self-centered or out-of-tune than a symptomatic person. You cannot function any-where near normal complaining of physical pains and frustra-tions that usually keep you symptomatic longer. SO NEVER COMPLAIN – EVER! Do not tell your family, friends, or staff of your symptoms. Make them secret (they like to find out your secrets). Do not worry – they know your weak-nesses and they know when you are physically down. Put it in your mind that you will not miss work, no matter what symptoms you exhibit.

NATURAL HEALING

"GOD DOES ALL HE DOES, BECAUSE HE IS ALL HE IS."

There is virtually nothing in our literature or in medical investigation regarding natural healing. We study the normal sequence of events regarding the process of healing; for example, surface wound healing. Perhaps this slow creative process is not sensational enough. This is not so for an Innate chiropractor though. There is that part of chiropractic that requires us to approach the subject more closely than any other profession. The fact that we neither add substances to nor subtract substances from the body only leads us to rely on Innate to bring about the natural, normal, sequential actions called natural healing.

Following Galileo's attempt to combine the physical and spiritual concepts in science, there has been an unwritten rule that science and religion become totally incompatible. Religion took the spiritual phenomenon, and medicine took over the physical actions. B.J. Palmer, however, took the other tack. His life was a constant morass of energies spent in the physical as well as the spiritual sciences. The point of emphasis is that medical science wants only tangible evidence and no spiritual values of the organism are correlated into the outcome. Religions suffer from too much escape. Some, such as the Roman Catholic Church, want more mystery, while others, like Christian Science, only want to dwell on the divinity of the human mind alone. Therefore, in scientific literature there is an absence of words such as "faith, feeling, intuition, revelation, or innate healing mechanisms." In religious literature, there is virtually no mention of the physical limitations of matter or healing by any other means than the spontaneous miracles which Jesus and the apostles performed. What B.J. wanted to do was combine both the spiritual and physical sciences into the powerful realization in chiropractic called natural healing. This is very difficult and problems arise where answers will never be forthcoming. Chiropractic is much better off in the purely scientific arena for definition and scope. The fact remains, however, that chiropractic must teach the philosophy of Innate healing and the principle of life. We must teach that. The "real" doctor is Innate Intelligence, and we mortal chiropractors merely "release" this natural healing intelligence by adjusting the subluxations. I personally find it hard to be anything but both physical and spiritual. I speak to my patients about mechanical concepts that coincide with the subluxation complex, but when I begin explaining the neuronal deficits, I shift the emphasis toward the degree of "time and force" necessary for natural healing. This constant effort will in time encourage every patient to consider the importance of their symptoms as they relate to corrections (adjustments).

I also believe that there are theologians willing to step forward and embrace our concepts. I have been in many discussions with ministers and have never, so far, seen one who was trained in seminary to understand man's healing principles or to correlate health concepts into religious doctrine. This parallels medical school in that chiropractic is never mentioned there nor are prayer and faith included in the medical model. It seems that we doctors and ministers tend to compartmentalize our lives and thinking. We want a spiritual compartment in which to put our mystical feelings about a supernatural God and have a health compartment relegated to a doctor or a pill made in a factory.

I am anxious for the scientific community to embrace serious investigation into the spiritual realm of healing and to begin the arduous task of training people to make sure that everything entering the oral cavity is organic foodstuff. This promotion and acceptance, coupled with the natural regimen and disciplines will lead one to understand the importance of mechanical alignment, neurological integrity, and spinal maintenance.

THE TECHNIQUE ERA

"THERE IS A PRINCIPLE WHICH IS AGAINST ALL INFORMATION, WHICH IS PROOF AGAINST ALL ARGU-MENT AND WHICH CANNOT FAIL TO KEEP MAN IN EVERLASTING IGNORANCE. THAT PRINCIPLE IS CON-DEMNATION BEFORE INVESTIGATION."
                                                    Spencer

In chiropractic college, we learn all the techniques available. Then, in student clinic, we begin to try our skills on patients. Usually we are so filled with information concerning the various techniques that we have not really learned which moves best fit our hands. We begin insulting these poor patients' spines with every move that we have learned, usually all at once! At the Palmer Clinic, we had patients who had let students work on them for so many years that we called these patients "Mr. Rubber Spine" or "Mr. Do Funny." I took care of several Mr. Rubber Spines and Mr. Do Funnies in student clinic. Soon it dawned on me that although it was necessary for me to tryout every move so that I could become familiar with it, it would be better to induce only one technique at a time until I found out which fit my hands best and what results followed each adjustment. Our technique instructors, Drs. Kern, Manaus, Palmer, and Phillips helped us during those long winter nights in clinic. I owe much thanks to these chiropractors. Also, Dr. Donald Pharoah is also responsible for giving me the concept of the "Touch and Tell" system that is detailed in Section II of this book.

When I began practice in Warsaw, Kentucky, in 1964, I was still "practicing" my techniques and modifying my Thompson, Gonstead and Palmer techniques to fit my hands. What happens is that eventually you settle into you routine technique after several years. "The New Zealand Report" had an interesting reference to a well-documented study that the chiropractor is at peak palpation and technique efficiency in the seventh year of practice. When I think back, I can relate to this concept. I feel, however, that each year I get a little better on my technique, and I always increase my "bag of tricks" each year to include successes I have had with a technique to a particular subluxation on a specific patient. I believe that this is how it should be. The most famous man with a "bag of moves" was Dr. Clarence Gonstead. "Ole G" made me realize that one of the greatest assets of being a chiropractor was the fact that you need never retire or lose your youthfulness in practice. When I was around Dr. Gonstead, I always felt that he was my senior only in knowledge and practice. When it came to chiropractic, he was always enthusiastic and young at heart. He told me his "secret" – the more patients you adjust and the more study you put into your technique, the more enthused you become to see new patients each day. In athletics, men and women gifted with great physical abilities arrive at their peak performance in a relatively short period of time. Age, however, soon forces the limelight to change to the younger players coming along. It is not so with chiropractors. Like the great athletes, however, I believe that there is a time in our youth when we need to say that we could do something with every fiber of our being and become the very best.

It is not important that you continue this forever because usually it is impossible. In order to get the gold medal, though, you need to know that at one time in your life you gave all the talent, dedication, time, sacrifice, and faith you had to accomplishing an important feat, and at that time, you adjusted as many patients as possible and were the best that you possibly could be. That is why you young practitioners need to concentrate on serving large volumes of patients and speaking your truths to the masses for the first ten years of your practice at least. My dad once told me long ago, to work day and night for the first ten years and then you will never have to do that again. What he meant, I found out later, was that there is physically no way to ever do what we did at that peak ten years ago. I know that I can never work as long and as hard as I did in the seventies. The challenge lies elsewhere for me now and continues to change with the times. Still, I will never forget what it took to see four hundred patients in one day. I also can never rest easy at night when I feel that I have "slacked" in my responsibilities. Not to have worked and achieved when it was possible to do so and to slack along in life reminds me that I am off course. Theodore Roosevelt once said, "Then you rank with those poor spirits who neither suffer much nor enjoy much, but rather live in that great twilight that knows not victory or defeat." I urge you on to victory.

The real technique era takes place after you have built a successful practice. Then you need to watch out for the time when you have your volume and income to the point that you become comfortable. You may begin to take in associates or get involved in hobbies that cause you to change your hours and tarnish your contact with your regular patients. When this happens, and you start rationalizing about your "slacking", the technique era begins. You wake up one day and the charts show a steady decline in volume and income. You get nervous and realize that you have to get back in the office and "pump" it up again. Sometimes you are smart and put those same success tools that got you up back into operation, such as the disciplines we have discussed in previous chapters.

Sometimes, though, the "comfort" has eroded your success disciplines so much that your ego convinces you that all you need is a new technique or a new piece of equipment. Soon you begin thinking that it is the quality of care, not the quantity, and you begin to doubt your established technique package that has been working fine until now. So you take a course and begin to dismiss patients or to change routine patients' technique. You may begin a stiff practice and treat patients like "bones." Soon what love you had for the patient and the bond you established over the years begins to unravel. If you catch this mistake and correct it in time, you can head off a technique era that could lead you further away from your real purpose of serving sick people.

These facts are true: the key is in service and in the doctor-patient esoterics that we have described here. All techniques work. Whenever I took new technique courses and tried them out, they all worked. My technique package included Palmer, Thompson, Gonstead, and Cox. After I saw the Activator research, and understood the tests, I wanted to correct subluxations with the high speed, low force adjustment. I had used the technique of low speed, high force for twenty years. Today I hold an Advanced Proficiency rated certificate from Activator Methods and use Activator Methods one-hundred percent in my practice. It has been an exciting challenge for me to move bones with the activator. The key here is to use a package which fits your style of practice and gets the patients well.

My advice to you is to keep technique in its proper perspective. Know that it is not the real reason that patients keep coming in year after year and sending in new patients. Please realize that your ego will try to trap you into thinking that you need a course on how to charge patients, decrease your volume and increase your fees. DO NOT fall into that trap.

You do need sound business management skills, but more important is the discipline and inspiration to keep you loving and serving your patients. You also need practice management for your staff plus weekly staff meetings and current charts of office statistics. I still believe, however, that it is more important to lose your grand and glorious SELF and to find that servant to humanity that you are supposed to be. Couple this with a strong desire and a supportive family and staff, and you have a practice that is fun as well as super successful.

STAYING UP

"NO ONE EVER DIED OF HARD WORK – BUT WORRY KILLS MILLIONS EVERY DAY."

Doctors who want to find out the secret of my success often ask me how I always "stay up." By this question, they are really telling me that they think life is a level of bliss that can last forever at some point. They want to know how they can get to that point, and quickly! This level (eternal bliss), however, is impossible unless you have reached perfection. I believe that only Jesus Christ is the perfect person. So, please understand, you need failures, blind alleys, and hopeless situations in order to GROW! If you have real tenacity, you can "fail your way to success!" By following the laws and being right on course, bliss comes along the way.

You must NOT live your life with the plateau concept of happiness. What I mean by this concept is thoughts which promote ideas like "as soon as I finish school," or "as soon as I get my doctorate," or "as soon as I get into practice," THEN I will be happy. By concentrating so much on the future, you scarcely make the moment enjoyable. I think that my big secret here is to try to give love every moment and to "bloom where I am right now." As a student, could you pick out the men and women who will become ultra-successful when they graduate? If you could, you also have some idea of exactly what qualities you saw in these people that you wanted to possess. You simply observed how they functioned day by day, and by this you could determine with much accuracy, how they will perform in the future. These people somehow seem to stay on course toward success. There are exceptions, of course, but it is different in chiropractic college than it was in high school or regular college. In high school, I am sure that we can all remember the star quarterback or the cheerleader who seemed to have it all "together" then but ended up as a failure when algebra gave way to real life! The success they had in school did not assure their continuing success. You do not ever have to be popular to be successful or to be a great humanitarian. You have to simply be willing to learn and apply. What you must do with your goal writing and affirmations is to include your happiness quota in them. How are you going to stay "up?" It is different for each one of us. Modest goals may mean that you are not fully putting yourself into what you are doing. Therefore, you go through each day with a mixture of joy, sadness, ecstasy and drudgery. This is the average for most people. To excel in day-to-day life is to look for the blissful moments and hang onto them. Savor them for as long as you can hold them. Learn to belly laugh every day. When you have a particularly full and busy day and it passes quickly, take inventory that evening when you are relaxing and recall the happiness created for you that day. In the morning, when it is prayer time, look for some present happiness or savor some past happiness. Nothing can be more inspiring and positive. You can guess that I am a nostalgic sentimentalist. I want to get as mushy as I can about almost any love thought or action. My only drawback, and probably yours, too, is that for some reason we seem to hold back the words and actions which would help us to share our bliss with someone else. If you can just keep yourself from holding back, then you can have a friend who can savor the joy with you! So, OPEN UP! LIGHTEN UP! Be vitally concerned about a happiness situation.

When a patient has great results and gets excited, go get your chiropractic assistant and anyone else who can also share the joy and enthusiasm. Get the patient to tell this person about his results. I often leave X-rays up on the view box and tell many patients about a successful case, until the excitement wears off. How about doing the same thing with your wife and children?

I bought my daughter a new car when she graduated from high school and you should have seen the excitement and joy that she displayed! I thought about this for many days, and it lasted over a month. In the same vein, my thirteen-year-old son saved all summer for a special bike – the Rolls Royce of freestyle bicycles. This expensive beauty had to be ordered piece by piece, and it was supposed to get here by Christmas. It had been back-ordered for some time, but the delivery service had a problem, so it did not get here until late on Christmas Eve. Mary Ann took him to pick it up when it finally did come, and I missed out on the first joy and excitement of the moment. When he showed me the bike later, he was still in "bliss city," but I missed the first wave and somehow felt cheated. I like to share happiness, but we must make the effort. When your patients testify, keep the excitement as long as possible.

A positive person does not always have to go around "hyped up." On the other hand, no one sees him negative either. You must be in the "zone" between the two levels. My advice is to never go into the adjusting room with a negative attitude. You must burst the ethers in that room when you do go in. My good friend, Joe Stucky, made it a habit in his clinic to literally "break down the door" when he came into an adjusting room. Try it some time and watch the startled looks on your patients' faces. The energy Joe exudes in each room is his way of "taking charge" and enhancing the healing mood in his office. Remember, if you go over negatives with a patient who has come in to build on your positive power, you will lose him. Also keep in mind the technique era of which we spoke earlier. You must not change the vibrations in the established patient. It is just as important not to take for granted what will happen if the bond of doctor/patient confidence is broken. That means new symptoms, life changes, whatever. You must be a whole-person doctor. In order to create the bedrock, lifetime patient, you must be up one hundred percent of the time, with each patient. It is the patients, ultimately, who make your professional life most valuable. Be thankful for them!

One final key on the "ups" is to find contentment in your times of frustrating thoughts and actions. This is the secret of balance. The loss of balance is ultimately more painful than giving up something that is required to maintain balance. If you are performing a task in your office or in your daily life which is constantly frustrating to do, use the following mental exercise: First ask yourself if you are getting lazy or complacent and just do not want to work at this task. Next, ask yourself who could do the task for you, or with whom could you share the thoughts that are frustrating you and thereby help resolve the frustration. My wife, Mary Ann, has to listen to me take out my frustrations. She is my best friend and does not take my frustrations seriously. Usually after I have released them, I feel considerably better even though Mary Ann may not be able to help me resolve the situation at all. Remember, any negative held inside will take the joy and enthusiasm out of life. This can allow a quality of subluxation to occur which brings Dis-Ease.

AMAZING CHIROPRACTIC STORIES

In Mississippi, we built the largest house in town. We also had a stable for more than twenty Tennessee Walking horses. We had various animals of every species, so I began the practice of adjusting my animals. Usually it was the atlas or the pelvis that I adjusted, but then there was "Oggie Doggie!" One of my patients is a veterinarian in Tupelo. He often discussed the pets he had seen with disk problems, and one day he called me to say that he had a bird dog which had jumped a fence with a leash on and had fractured his fifth cervical vertebra. The dog was totally paralyzed and had no movement or reflexes of any kind. The owner had asked the vet to put the dog to sleep. The vet asked the man if he could have the dog to observe and the owner agreed. He then called me, and I went down to his office. On the way I remembered a story that Dr. Gonstead had once told me about a chiropractor who had fractured his third cervical vertebra in a motorcycle accident. This chiropractor was flown into Mount Horeb. Dr. Gonstead said that he X-rayed and adjusted the axis and third cervical vertebrae and then sandbagged the patient. He only adjusted this patient three or four times before the patient started responding. In six months, the man went from being a quadriplegic to being able to practice in his own office. Dr. Gonstead believed that the hemorrhage at the cord level is unresolved in medical care. Innate cannot move the blood out of the neural canal because there is a subluxation. Once the necrosis begins at the fracture site it destroys the cord, resulting in more necrosis and eventually permanent paralysis. Dr.

Gonstead believed that the adjustment not only aligned the vertebrae, but restored circulation that allowed Innate to resolve the hemorrhage as well as the necrosis.

When I got to the vet's office and saw the dog, we took some more X-rays, and the vertebra above the fracture was the vertebra that appeared to be dislocated, it was so misaligned. When I rotated the cervical spine to be adjusted, I heard all kinds of weird crepitation – "grinding and popping." The dog just looked at me so I continued the adjustment with those "Oggie Doggie" eyes staring at me. C4 adjusted just like a human's spine, and we then put the dog back into his cage. My own dogs were always hard to adjust because the ligaments always seemed so tight, but not so with that dog. I went down to the vet's office and adjusted the dog two more times. In about a week, the vet called me and said that the dog was moving one foot. From that point on, the dog gradually recovered all movement, and by the next winter, he was hunting in the field! I also adjusted dogs with disk problems, with one hundred percent results, but this was the first fracture case that I had ever seen, and the results were amazing. I think of all the paraplegics who could possibly benefit from adjustments if there could be some integrated research on adjustments and vertebral fractures. I know that if I had a spinal fracture with or without neurological deficit, I would not hesitate to get a specific chiropractic adjustment.

BIG JIM

One day in my office in Mississippi, a lady was telling me about her thirty-year-old son who was retarded, would not speak and had never gone to school. She said that he was normal until age five, when he was rocking in a chair on the porch. The rocking chair turned over, and he fell off the porch backwards, landing on his neck and head. He deteriorated mentally from that day on and gradually stopped talking completely. I got her to bring "Big Jim" to see me, and he was definitely a big man. He was well over six feet tall and was very large boned. The X-rays revealed an extremely inferior atlas and on motion, the upper cervicals were completely fixed on cervical extension. I adjusted him for several months and he gradually began to show signs of "waking up" to his capacities. He started talking and eventually went to school. The family was told that he had a very high IQ. He finally got a job and became a real person again. I like unusual cases, and for some reason, have never shied away from them, no matter how serious the condition. I truly believe that chiropractic offers something for hopeless cases.

THE DIERFIELD LEG TEST

I met Romie Dierfield at Homecoming in 1961. My good friend, David Hughes and I were looking at the new adjusting tables on display. Romie came up behind us and began asking questions about our college work. Later he asked us if we knew the Dierfield leg check. We were both very active in Thompson technique and this is the fundamental test for Thompson work. He then introduced himself and we were really impressed.

Dr. Dierfield was very old. He was stoop-shouldered and was walking with a cane. What took our attention was his nose. The nasal septum was missing, and what tissue there was, was down deep in the nasal cavity. Dr. Dierfield told David and me that one day he was giving an adjustment when the phone rang. He was his own assistant, so he picked up the phone. While he was talking, the patient on the table picked up her head and turned it to look to one side. Dr. Dierfield noticed her leg pull up short. When she put her head down straight, the legs evened. From this observation, he developed the now famous Dierfield leg test.

Dr. Dierfield told us that at first, he would not teach this discovery to anyone, because he wanted to pass it along to his son. Later he developed a melanoma on his nose and was on his deathbed, when he called B.J. and asked him to come see him because he wanted to tell B.J. about his discovery. He told us that as soon as B.J. became fully knowledgeable about the test, his cancer went into remission and that had been many years ago. Dr. Dierfield left us as mysteriously as he had appeared, but I will never forget this dedicated chiropractor and his amazing story!

BEBOUT COLLEGE

Dr. Earl Bebout was a short, feisty chiropractor. When Bill King and I would drive to Palmer, we always went through Indianapolis, Indiana where the little red brick house with the neon sign stood. The sign said "Bebout College of Chiropractic." Bill always wanted to stop. One day, we did stop and the old man met us at the door. He was excited that we were Palmer students and he went on and on about his respect for B.J. Dr. Bebout graduated from Palmer College of Chiropractic in the 1920s and we could never tell if he had any students in his "school." We never saw any that day. Dr. Bebout showed us around the entire school, which was also his office. When we were finished, I made the mistake of asking him about his X-ray department. He turned red in the face and started cursing X-rays. He said that he broke with B.J. over X-rays. "Besides," he said, "if Jesus Christ did not need X-rays to heal people, then chiropractors did not need them either!" We were impressionable students at the time, and we were a little stunned. Next, Dr. Bebout got Bill down on his hi-lo adjusting table to show him the Bebout technique. It was all spinus process contacts with a very FORCEFUL recoil. Bill's head and legs would fly up in the air, and he would cry out! Dr. Bebout tried to get me down, but I refused. Much later, I heard Dr. Bebout speak in Atlanta. He still burned with the fire of his convictions, and he still loved chiropractic as much as I have ever seen a chiropractor love his profession.

Dr. J. CLAY THOMPSON

The King chiropractors all had Palmer and Thompson adjusting tables. Bill introduced me to Dr. J. Clay Thompson when we got to Davenport, and right away, Clay started "selling" me his table. I bought my first one when I was in twelfth quarter. Later Clay told us to come work with him in his office on Harrison Street.

When I first saw Clay adjust a patient, I noticed that he adjusted almost every vertebra. Then he adjusted the ribs, anterior pelvis and AC joints. Finally he worked on the knees and feet! What is left?! He had more "moves" than I could learn! Clay was always way ahead of his time in building adjusting equipment, but he could not sit still long enough to write down his technique! Finally Dr. Joe Stucky wrote the technique manual and got Clay teaching consistently. There has never been anyone whom I have met in chiropractic who could move bones as fast as Clay did. He had to develop the pneumatic table, because his leg would go numb, pumping the old manual cocking tables! Then he put the automatic return on the pelvic section and he was in high speed, rapid fire! He looked like a semi-automatic weapon when he adjusted the pelvis! I used Thompson tables for twenty years and I am sure that everyone who has ever used his table was as proud of this fine equipment as they were proud to know J. Clay. God bless you Peggy and Clay.

CHILD'S PLAY

In Tupelo, Mississippi there is a large children's home. It is called "The Children's Mansion" and the main building with its majestic southern columns truly casts this appearance. However, behind those walls are sixty plus children who have seen and experienced lifetimes of mental and physical trauma, in only a few short years of life. The director, Reverend Stephen Drury, with his wife, Evelyn and their dedicated staff, put one hundred per cent of their love and energy into these kids. I have served, but not anywhere close to the twenty-four hour a day, three hundred and sixty-five days a year duty that these people put in. When I look at these men and women, I think of the command of Jesus to "feed my sheep."

One crisp autumn day, I had a call from the Mansion, because I had an article about a bed wetter in the Tupelo Daily Journal. Every Monday morning for many years, I ran a chiropractic testimonial. No medical doctor in town liked it, but no one could argue with a cured case!

The lady on the phone told Mary Ann that she had nine chronic bed wetters at the Mansion. We told her to keep records, because I was going to work. I was convinced that the segments two and three of the sacrum were subluxated, along with the fourth lumbar and twelfth thoracic. I also believed that no matter what mental or physical trauma had been inflicted on these children, that I could correct these subluxations. I adjusted nine children. Innate cured seven of these. They invited me to supper one evening and I brought my portable adjusting table. I adjusted the entire staff. Twenty one years later, the doctor who bought my practice in Mississippi, still takes care of the kids at the Mansion! Thanks Dr. Brewer and thanks, Reverend Steve.

THE GOVERNOR'S CHIROPRACTOR

When I set out to get a chiropractic licensing law passed in Mississippi, I knew that I would have to know a lot of state politicians. One of my goals was to be the Governor's chiropractor. I would find out when my candidate would be in Tupelo and I would go down to the hotel to meet him and give him a check for the enormous campaign expenses all candidates face. In general, I tried to convince each candidate that I wanted to do all I could to help him get elected. I was surprised at how desperately all of them needed friends and support. That is when I learned the first rule of politics "Never desert your friends." I did not know any of the candidates personally at first, but I had some patients, Reese Senter and Grady Smith who had been involved in Mississippi politics for many years. I borrowed their enthusiasm for the candidates which they supported. We picked Governor Bill Waller and Lt. Governor Cliff Finch. Bill beat everyone in the primary and became one of Mississippi's best chief executives. He signed the chiropractic licensing act into law in 1973. Cliff Finch lost in the primary. When I was asked what these men could do for me, I told them that I wanted to be the governor's chiropractor. No governor could run for a second term in Mississippi, so in four years, Cliff Finch came to me for help. He wanted to become Governor this time, but no one had much faith in his efforts. He was a crazy guy, but I really liked him, and I believe that he liked me. I started adjusting him right away. He went on to beat all the odds and became our next governor! He called me to the Governor's Mansion to adjust him. I also adjusted him in Reese's home, in my own home, in my office and at the state capitol. It was fun!

Whenever there was chiropractic legislation or information needed, Cliff always called me first. He never forgot that I had helped him at a time when no one else would. He also appointed me to my second term of five years which I served on the Mississippi State Board of Chiropractic Examiners. I was fortunate enough to pick the next governor also, who appointed me to a third consecutive term on the Board of Examiners. However, Governor Finch was my favorite governor.

THE GREAT LEADER

"IF YOU DID IT, IT IS NOT FROM GOD. IF YOU CAN BRAG ON IT, IT IS NOT GRACE."
Pastor Teacher Gene Cunningham

Every Wednesday night at 9:00 there were ten to fifteen chiropractors who would come to my clinic for a meeting. I would adjust them and several would watch me adjust my last few patients that night. Then I would lead a class. We would usually go over some office procedures and then have discussion as well as a question and answer session. Later, we would go out to eat and have more fellowship. It was a great time in my life.

Many of these people were men and women whom I had encouraged to come to Mississippi to practice. Some of them had worked for me. I was their leader, teacher, and mentor. So I thought!

One such doctor was Noal Rossow. I met Noal at one of the meetings in Davenport when I lectured to two hundred or more students. Then they all went home and got their families, and came back to get adjusted. I adjusted a few hundred students and family members before I left that night.

I remember Noal well. He sat up front. He was older than I was and his wife Claire was usually home with the kids. Noal told me he came to Palmer because of Claire and her family. When Claire was a little girl, her parents would pack a picnic lunch and go to Mount Horeb to see Dr. Gonstead. They would leave home well before dawn, so that they could sign in by 7:00 A.M. and see Dr. Gonstead. Then they would go to the park for lunch, while they took turns watching the sign in list. Some time after noon, they would get their turn and go in to see Dr. Gonstead. Dr. Gonstead adjusted them all in one room. No one had X-rays. They would get home after dark. Claire always had a lot of enthusiasm for chiropractic. Noal was quiet and reserved. I liked this family right away and they came to hear me speak at the D.E. meetings in Atlanta when Noal was a student. After graduation, Noal came to my clinic and asked me about a location. I knew that he needed a small town to start out in and suggested the quiet little town of Pontotoc, Mississippi. Noal, Claire and their lovely family were an "instant success" in Pontotoc. I was proud of being able to help them.

Later, Noal told me his story. In Davenport, his confidence was low and he was thinking about dropping out of chiropractic school. Then he heard about my lecture and decided to go. After listening to me talk for several hours, a positive thought struck him and he made a firm resolve in his heart to keep on with chiropractic. The thought was "If someone like Tom Morgan, who obviously cannot talk without mumbling, has no striking features, and does not really impress me, can be successful in this profession, then with all I have going for me, in the way of business experience SURELY I can make a bigger success than this man!"

So, my bubble was bursted! I decided to quit trying to act like somebody important, and start giving God the credit for placing me in the right place at the right time, for sending me such a dedicated and sincere marriage partner, and most importantly for giving me the ability to stick with my practice morning and night without complaint and without laziness.

So, if you are impressed with yourself now, there is a Noal Rossow out there somewhere gaining confidence and getting ideas from what you are NOT.

The trick is to let your ego go and then go to work today! Trying hard to do something for someone else without thinking about yourself, your problems or your successes, is also a key. Stay positive in the face of negativity for only God brings this peace called grace. Then it passes all understanding.

CHARLOTTE

Shirley Bowen presented in our office as a last resort. She had the flu every winter and her resistance was at an all time low. She was going to have to give up her job as a grade school teacher. Shirley had polio as a child and wore a leg brace. Her pelvis, like her leg, was small and malformed. Her strength was very low. Only her strong will to go to school each day, and the encouragement she received from her family, kept her alive. She was helped back to the X-ray room by her mother Erdice and her Aunt Shirley. She could only stand up for short periods of time. After receiving her first adjustment, she began to get stronger. Her colds and flu symptoms abated and her eyes began to take on new brightness. She was coming back to life. Shirley came for her adjustments three times a week for four or five years. Many weeks, I adjusted her every day. Her cervical spine was one of the most difficult I have ever adjusted, but it was also the site of her primary subluxations.

One day she told me that she was pregnant. She had had several miscarriages and the obstetrician told her that it was because her pelvis was so atrophied and malformed. They had told her that she would never be able to carry a baby to term. Shirley came to me faithfully for nine months and today, her only child "Charlotte" is a very healthy teenager. No doctor knows what Innate can or cannot do. The human body is an amazing organism and the longer I stay in practice, the greater respect I have for the healing capabilities of Innate Intelligence. Shirley taught me never to give up – Innate never does!

THE KIDNEY MACHINE

John came to our office with an interesting story. One of my patients who was a registered nurse at the Tupelo hospital, referred John to me. When he was presented for care, he had two IVs in each arm. He was jaundiced, underweight and could hardly sit up. He said that both of his kidneys had been removed because of tumors. He was undergoing dialysis every day, but it was catching up with him. He had been given from three to six months to live.

John said that his back was so painful that he could not sleep or move around. The X-rays revealed a wedge at T11 and T12. It reminded me of the subluxation picture in our literature which was supposed to have been taken from an actual X-ray of a person who had died with kidney disease.

I told John about the subluxation and adjusted him. He returned a couple of days later and said that his back pain was some better. I gave him another adjustment, and after that I never saw John again. It was a sad case.

One day though, about four or five months later, Mary Ann came back to call me out of the adjusting room. She said to come quickly to the front. When I got there, John was there smiling at me. He looked familiar, but I had no idea who he was. He kept saying "Don't you remember me?" Well, my memory for names is not the best, so finally he said that he was playing a joke on me. He also told me that the last time I had seen him, he was twenty-five pounds thinner and near death! Then he related that after his last adjustment at our office, he went back to the hospital. They always checked his blood pressure before he was put on the dialysis machine. His blood pressure had always been over 200 systolic, so he had been rejected as a candidate for kidney transplant. However, when they took his blood pressure this time it was 120/80! He was flown from Tupelo to the Medical Center in Jackson and a kidney transplant was performed the next day. John is still alive to my knowledge and he came in for adjustments for many years while I was in Tupelo.

DRAKE

I was sitting by the swimming pool at the downtown Marriott Hotel in Atlanta with several friends, when someone pointed out that there was a boy lying on the bottom of the pool, and that he had been there for some time. We pulled Drake Hughes up on the apron of the pool. His dad, David, was my best friend in college and now we were standing together looking hopelessly at his son and the lifeguard trying frantically to resuscitate the child. There was no response. David and I pounced on the boy and began our own resuscitation. Still, no response. On the spur of the moment, I asked David what Drake's atlas listing was. He told me and I adjusted him. The instant his atlas moved, Drake spit up water and began to sputter and revive. He did not have much water in him, so we thought that he might have hit his head on the bottom of the pool. Today, Drake is in chiropractic college! The longer I practice, the greater is my belief in the far reaching need for chiropractic adjustments. Biomechanical integrity, with its spinal neuronal component must be a priority in trauma centers. Today, we often hear of untrained orthopedists telling patients that "It is only a sprain." In fact, only the chiropractor and the chiropractic patient know the path to getting that patient to the pre-accident level. We have only really touched the tip of the iceberg when it comes to understanding the full ramifications of the vertebral adjustment.

STROKING OUT

One night a patient called me about his wife who was a patient. He wanted me to come over to her house and adjust her. She had a migraine headache and was dizzy and nauseated.

When I got to her home, she was in bed with her eyes rolled back in her head! She was mumbling unintelligibly and moving her head from side to side. Her husband almost had to be resuscitated himself! After I got the family out of the room, I put the blood pressure cuff on her arm to take the blood pressure. It was at the very top at 260! Well, I knew that she was having a cardiovascular accident, so I did what I always do in emergencies. I looked at her atlas listing and got up in the bed with her to adjust her atlas. When I got down and sat on the side of the bed, I saw her eyes straighten up. She looked like one of my daughter's dolls, that when you lay them back, their eyes move! The cuff was still on her arm, so I checked her blood pressure again. This time, it was 120/80. I checked it three times and it was still 120/80! She was actually sleeping peacefully by now, so I just sat and stared at my patient for a couple of hours, checking her blood pressure frequently.

Her vital signs were all normal, so finally I went home. The next day, she came walking into my office. I never told her what had happened, but only thanked God for chiropractic and His healing power.

MY HARVEY LILLIARD STORY

Every chiropractor adjusts patient after patient, year after year. There are many interesting cases, but mostly, like life, practice is repetitive. Then, a Harvey Lilliard case walks into your office! Moving bones year after year, got me my "Harvey." God must have thought that I was ready!

Jane was blind in one eye. She had chronic sinus problems and headaches. When I examined her and X-rayed her, she had the spinus of axis rotated ten millimeters to the left. The cervical scoliosis was to the right and it was a most unusual neck.

After I did a Thompson move on the left axis spinus, she took her file and headed down the hall to the front desk. All of a sudden I heard someone screaming, "I can see, I can see!!" She was crying and hugging Mary Ann. Then she began going into other adjusting rooms and telling other patients about her miracle. She had been blind in that eye for twenty years! I ran her testimonial in the newspaper on Monday morning. Jane said to be sure to put her phone number in the ad, and she had many calls. I had many patients! So, chiropractors, look out! One of these days, Harvey Lilliard is coming!

(In 1895, Harvey Lilliard was the first chiropractic patient. He had been deaf in one ear for twenty years. Dr. D.D. Palmer adjusted his neck and his hearing was restored).

SPECIAL FRIENDS

In practice, one comes in contact with very special people. In a relatively short time, these people put their trust in you and become your special friends. As these patients come in year after year, the "family" practice soon develops which brings a stability that I believe cannot be achieved in other professions. I would like to relate a little about some of the "special" friendships which developed in my practices, both in Kentucky and Mississippi.

Silas Ratliff was in his late eighties when he began chiropractic care. He was a black man whose first impression on me told me that I was dealing with a very intellectual person. I had very few black patients in Mississippi, when I was first in practice there. Being a product of the 60s, I was deeply interested in individual rights and freedoms. Silas and I talked many times of the oppression blacks were forced to endure in the south, and how this compared to chiropractic oppression by the medical organizations. Silas was the principal in the black high school in Tupelo before integration. He was probably one of the most respected Tupeloans of any race. When integration forced its way south, Tupelo had already integrated and Silas was co-principal at this time. Many people told me that Silas almost single handedly caused Tupelo to integrate without an incident, BEFORE the civil rights legislation! Silas came in every week for adjustments and referred many of his friends and family to me for care. He kept up his adjustments on a regular basis, until he became bedridden and could no longer go out. He was in his mid nineties at that time. One Christmas, my chiropractic assistant, Peggy Hamilton, suggested that our "something special" for that Christmas could be visiting our elderly patients and bringing them baked goods and presents. Peggy, Jean, and Mary Ann got up a list of people to see, and then they made lots of cookies and candies. We divided these up into boxes which were brightly wrapped and decorated for distribution to our "special friends." When we got to Silas's house, he was nearly an invalid at that time. Even so, he was still dressed in a white shirt and tie. I felt a special presence in his little home and his wife made us feel very welcome as she talked about how Silas believed chiropractic to be the most progressive health profession for the future. I was looking at some of his pictures on the walls, and I asked him this question: "What advice would you give a young man just starting out in life?" Without hesitation, he said he would recommend "Perseverance ... our greatest gift. I would tell him to row the row real high, and only look straight ahead – never left or right, and never cease walking straight." He went on to tell me that his father was a farmer, and when they broke new ground, it was Silas's job to drive the stake at the far end of the field and tie his handkerchief around it. Then, when his dad would plow the row, he would aim his horse straight at the stake with the handkerchief. His dad made sure never to take his eyes off the stake. If he even once looked back to see if his row was straight, that was when the row would waver.

Silas also told me that this was his dad's sole advice to him as a young man. It made me wonder how many pupils in whom Silas later instilled this "straight" philosophy. I never saw Silas again after that, but I never forgot him.

THE GALLATIN COUNTY NEWS

Charlie Adams was a tall, slow talking, small-town newspaperman. I rented my first office from him in Warsaw, Kentucky for sixty-five dollars per month. I still remember his eight foot line-o-type machine clicking through the walls of my adjusting room every Tuesday and Wednesday. Charlie was like many of those people you meet when you are first starting out. You like him right away and somehow the chemistry is right, and he cannot do enough for you.

Charlie laid out my Open House ads for his newspaper, and when the big day came, I had ads on every page of his weekly paper, and the middle spread!! You would have thought that Albert Schweitzer was opening up!! My Open House was a great success. We had sixty people to tour my office that afternoon in a town of eight hundred! Charlie told me to hurry up and cure a few folks so he could spread the word. And believe me ... the word spread quickly. I told Charlie to go out and bring me the sickest, most influential citizen in Warsaw. The next morning, he met me at the door of my office with one of his 7:00 a.m. coffee buddies. Mr. Wilson was the many generation owner of the Wilson Lumber Company. He had shingles all over his face. He was bandaged because the affected areas were so close to his eyes and the medical doctor had told him that they were getting into his eyes. He said that he was nearly blind in one eye at this time. I set him in front of my Picker field unit and took three cervical views. The atlas vertebra was lateral right. I put Mr. Wilson down on the Thompson table and adjusted his sixth dorsal vertebra, as well as toggling his atlas, ASRA. I read him twice a day on the NCGH and adjusted him several more times. In four days, his eye cleared up and you could tell that the lesions were digressing. He was on demurol for pain and he had been able to reduce his medication by half! Well, you know the rest of the story. The shingles cleared and Mr. Wilson was my first miracle in Warsaw. The word spread throughout the town and my practice took off. Mr. Wilson came to me regularly all four years that I stayed in Warsaw. Charlie Adams was always my good friend and patient, too. I shall never forget such a true friend.

Elsie Weldon was my first chiropractic assistant. I told Charlie to help me find the most respected citizen in town. He said that I needed one who would also be a good gossip! Elsie fit the bill and was a great chiropractic assistant. She knew everyone and was not hesitant to bring all her family and friends in to meet "her" doctor. Soon, I had a Weldon family practice! Others who helped me much in the early days in Warsaw were Ulous Carlton, Dora and Claude Ritch, and hundreds of others. These people helped make my years there filled with love and service.

Reese Senter was my best friend in Mississippi. I owe most of my success there to this man. His faith in me never changed from the first day that I met him. Dr. Ferrell Pittman and I went to Palmer College together. Ferrell was practicing in Columbus, Mississippi which was about forty miles from Tupelo. When I stopped to see the Pittmans in 1968, Ferrell told me about Reese Senter, and how he was driving eighty miles a day so that his wife could go to Ferrell in Columbus. When I went to see Reese, he took Mary Ann and I around the area, and showed us his construction and concrete company. He told me to pick out a lot that I liked, and he would build me a clinic. All I had to do was pay the first month's rent when I opened up! I went home and sold my practice in Kentucky and moved to Mississippi. I knew that I had gone as far as possible in Warsaw. The Tupelo-Verona area was about forty thousand in population – just the size town for which I was looking. Reese eventually sold me the clinic after I started rolling. He also later sold me the land where we had our home and farm. What a guy! He took me to many political meetings with him and got me on the governor's staff as well as helping me get on the first Board of Chiropractic Examiners in Mississippi. You name it, and Reese could not do enough to help me. Thanks Reese.

I also remember my many faithful patients who came every week for fifteen years. Some of them are Fessie and Becky Pennington, John Gober, Elva Stephenson and Shirley Bowen. I also had some patients who helped me get started in politics – Grady Smith and LeRoy Belk. I also fondly remember Mrs. Johnson who lived next door to my clinic for many years. Although she never became a patient herself, she faithfully sent me anywhere from two to five patients a week. She told everyone, "It doesn't matter what you have, just come on over and Dr. Morgan can help you!"

I was the first doctor of chiropractic in my family. My father told me that the only other doctor in our family was his grandfather, who was a medical doctor and supposedly helped found the first hospital in Cedartown, Georgia. One of my proudest times is when a relative tells me that he or she wants to become a chiropractor. I know that whenever someone has what it takes to make a decision like that, much faith and happiness will be added to a subluxated world. My cousins, Drs. Bob and Kay Schilling in New Castle, Pennsylvania are chiropractors, as is my brother-in-law Dr. Charlie Kalb in Atlanta, Georgia. My other cousins, Drs. David and Joyce Middendorf are chiropractors in Seattle, Washington. Two of my patients chose to become chiropractors, Dr. Herbert Brewer in Verona, Mississippi and Dr. David Ritch, in Fulton, Mississippi. Other acquaintances whom I influenced to go to chiropractic college are Dr. Mike Masterson in Strongsville, Ohio and Dr. Steve Amadeo in Collierville, Tennessee.

We have come full circle now, for our daughter Amy Charlotte, is presently in her second trimester at Palmer. Our oldest son Tom is a senior at Appalachian State and will receive his bachelor of science before going on to Palmer for his D.C. degree. Our youngest son, Jack is a senior in high school, here at McEachern and he also says he will study to become a chiropractor.

THE BIG GOAL

"THERE IS NO HONOR IN GIVING UP WHAT YOU CANNOT KEEP, TO GAIN WHAT YOU CANNOT LOSE."

When I was in my second quarter, I made up my mind that I would believe in and try out this chiropractic to its fullest. I vowed to myself that I would never take a pill or shot for the rest of my life unless I was involved in trauma. Mary Ann and I later set the same goal for our children. If the secret to health is Innate inside each one, then proper adjustments and daily regimen, would be all we need to do to keep our bodies in normal function (health). I have a twenty-year-old daughter who has only had a fever one time in her life. It only lasted about one hour. That sounds unbelievable, even to write it down, but it is true nonetheless.

Our two boys have had lots of fevers, but none of them ever got out of control because of chiropractic adjustments. I am thankful that none of us has ever been to a medical doctor's office or had a shot or pill. Jack did hit a car once while riding his motorcycle and had to have twenty-four stitches in his lip, but that was in the emergency room, and he needed no pain pills afterwards. I used first aid well and used a lot of butterfly bandages on our children. It is not easy getting through life without a pill. A pure bloodstream must be a high-priority item!

Mary Ann told me the other day that she asked our oldest son, Tommy, if he had ever tried drugs with his friends. He laughed and said that he had made it for twenty-one years without a pill, so why would he start now?! I want to believe that children really do learn from their models, even though they have a free will and can decide right or wrong for themselves. I pray that the kids will always try to do what is right.

In high school and college, I always had my own band. While at Palmer, we played at Rock Island on the weekends and on the riverboat every Thursday night. Since my Davenport days, I have had many songs come through, and I continue to write songs for a hobby. Actually God brings the songs to me and I try to remember to write them down. In 1971, I recorded a song for Life Foundation that I had written in 1968. We recorded it on a private label and sold the records to raise money for the Life Mobile Unit. It was never a number one hit, but it pretty well told the message. It is called "The Father Inside". It goes like this:

"As a young man, I see my son standing by my knee
And I wonder what he'll become when he's as old as me
I might not be around then to decide
So he must know where his faith comes from
I taught him. It comes from inside.
When you were younger, son, you called me "Dad"
And all that ever was, in me did you depend
But you've grown older now boy, so you must realize
There is a greater father than me, it's the father inside.

I tried to bring you up depending on the Father inside.
The Power that makes your heart beat and breathes your
    life.
If you've gained this wisdom, son, then all my work is
    through

For when you leave home, you take along,
The Father inside of you.

You come to your mom and me and say you've found
    a wife
A girl who understands that the power inside is her
    life
You say she does not depend on you or anything
But only in the power called life,
That the knowledge of the spirit brings.

And so the years go by and your mom and I must leave.
There'll be no sadness son, there'll be no time to grieve.
For you will understand that God has called us home
And you must love and trust His will
For the Father always knows."

Copyright 1971 T. O. Morgan, D.C.

BURNOUT

*"IF YOU DON'T GET WHAT YOU WANT ... IT'S A SIGN
THAT YOU DIDN'T SERIOUSLY WANT IT – OR YOU
TRIED TO BARGAIN OVER THE PRICE."*
Rudyard Kipling

Before we talk about my burnout, let us develop some inward
questions to ask yourself. Write down your answers, and be
honest with yourself. If you have not yet been in practice for
ten years, you may proceed to the next chapter.

Do you feel that you have to push yourself each day, week
or month to succeed? Do you have to prove your success
story over and over? Could it be that this attitude is really
bringing you down instead of keeping you up? Just what is
the stress of success telling you at this moment? What about
your free time? Do you have to generate excitement again
and again in order to keep yourself from being bored? You
must ask yourself if one area of your life consumes you, even
though you could be exploring other interests. Do you lack
intimacy with people around you? Are you unable to relax,
really take off a day for no particular reason, now that you
have succeeded in your practice? Do you have to always be
RIGHT? Do you constantly have to preserve your image?
Do you shift your goals back and forth between long-range
or short-range goals?

Now write down some more answers – make sure you are
clear to yourself on these. Probably the most important question

is "Is this how I want to be?" Is your present condition the way you started out being? Only you can know when it is time to quit driving yourself. Only you can know when your resources and abilities have become depleted. However, in order to take the DEEP look inside yourself, you have to become aware of and admit those feelings and realities. My problem was that at burnout time, I was very hard on myself. I simply could not admit that I might possibly be "burned out" on something that had given me so much pleasure and intensity in my life. I did not want to face the fact that perhaps I had accomplished so much so quickly that it might actually be time to take stock, relax, and have some other type of fun for a change. No wonder some average treatments for burnout are alcohol, gambling, sexuality, and other false cures. I was inwardly rebuking myself for not doing more, achieving more, being more. I simply could not slow down my intensity, even though my innermost feelings were telling me to do this.

Burnout does not last forever. The key here is change – positive or negative, forward or backward. If it is burnout time, you must make a positive change or change will come in a detrimental fashion. Now is the time to re-assess your goals in terms of their intrinsic worth. Get out of your "stuck" zone and update your attitude. Find the little kid in yourself, pat yourself on the head and say "Everything will be okay." Get out of the habit of placing blame on others. Think about your practice. Are you letting it devour you? Can you continue to do a good job without being so intense? Can you really take a day off now and then and really relax? Maybe you need to actually "work" at relaxing. I know I do. My recommendation is to first take a quick survey of how you spend your time. Have you let your social life deteriorate into nothingness? What about your old friends or finding new ones? After you once become successful in practice and level out, the key is to try to establish a well-rounded life. If you spend seventy-five percent of your energy in practice, make sure you are in that practice seventy-five percent of the time, with one hundred per cent dedication, desire, and discipline. The twenty-five percent with family or leisure activities should also encompass the same three motivations of dedication, desire and discipline. I found that it takes real effort for me to relax, and to take part in family activities, but it must be done.

I never wanted to say that I was "burned out" in practice, but it was true. Burnout comes from many things and for several reasons. Hindsight tells me that my time for burnout came at mid-life when all of my wildest practice goals, as well as state and national political goals, had been fulfilled. It was time to move on, not to burn out. I should have taken two years off from practice, taken a sabbatical, and then returned to practice. I never understood the security that having a good practice brings until I stayed out for two years. Having patients who depend on you on a regular basis also does much for your peacefulness. However, you have to be ready and able to serve, and when you go through a certain period of time in your life, you should get out of practice until you are in line and can once again appreciate the patients. The key here is that complacency erodes your destiny and your will. How do we become complacent?

My last day in practice in Verona, Mississippi was a Saturday morning and I adjusted one hundred and ten patients before I drove to Atlanta for the final time. The symptoms of burnout followed me to Georgia. Here are some relatives:

- You do not want to see new patients.
- You do not think you need any new patients.
- You do not want to talk to your patients who call at home.

- You begin to complain about your symptoms and your practice.
- You want to shorten your hours and raise your fees.
- You begin to think you are in competition with other chiropractors in the area.
- Your monthly bills take on a new meaning – BURDEN.
- You become moody and irritable with patients and family.
- You begin to look to the outside to things and people for strength.

When you cannot get up in the morning and do your affirmations and look forward to a day of service, you have problems. If you have a successful practice and have practiced for ten or fifteen years, you do not have to think about what made the practice go in the first place. However, it was your dedication, desire, and discipline. Suddenly, by osmosis, you begin to let the three "D's" erode. Then it is burnout time.

Burnout, however, should never be used as an excuse to explain a failing practice. If this is what you are attempting to do, it is not burnout. There is another problem within you for that one. Burnout comes while you are still holding up the practice and your life. It comes when your goals have been met and when comfort has taken a front seat in your life. When your practice is at a peak, SELL IT!

Another way to handle a burnout situation is to find another chiropractor and draw up a contract with this person for either one or two years. Then he or she can take over your practice for this period of time and know that when it is over, he or she will leave. You must make the contract of benefit to the new doctor. Your job is to take a sabbatical and seek areas of interest that can provide you with a needed rest, new goals, and new growth.

Another way to deal with this problem is to hire an associate, cut your hours down, travel, and end your contact with patients. Having an associate also allows you to take time off for longer periods of time when necessary for rejuvenation. I always wanted to teach at Life Chiropractic College. Mary Ann and I donated the first ten thousand dollars that went to start the new college in 1973. A part of me yearned to be part of the great experience at Life Chiropractic College. When the opportunity to sell my practice presented itself, I began to test the move. I had my house and farm in Verona appraised for two hundred and fifty thousand dollars. I sold it in nine days! The same thing happened with the ten rental units that we owned. I sold my clinic and my practice in the same month and we moved to Atlanta.

After nearly two years at the school, I resigned and opened a practice in the Austell area near Atlanta. That is when I realized just how stabilizing a practice was. The students at Life College are still very close to my heart, though, and I enjoyed sharing my knowledge and experience with them. I hope to return to teaching some day. However, I simply could not figure out how much I really missed helping people get well and teaching them about chiropractic. Only a practice allows you to do this. It was fun to reach back into the past and remember how I started a practice years ago, to see if the success formula would work again. The first month I had more than one hundred new patients, and my biggest day was fifty-three visits. It has been a fun and exciting challenge. I would never have "thunk" it!!! It took me those two years to get my enthusiasm back for practicing.

My advice to you would be to study the questions and your answers to the symptoms listed above and decide if you are going to rededicate yourself or take a sabbatical from practice. Either way, you have to keep writing down goals that keep you serving and growing. Some of my new goals are to write these pages that you are now reading. This is the model and the theme that I wanted to give the students at Life College. I want to help new doctors just starting out in practice, and I want to do all I can to preserve the chiropractic heritage and see that its purity is perpetuated. I also want to help patients get better and get the "Big Idea". For the present, I want to begin the beginning again and continue to grow mentally, spiritually, and physically.

CHIROPRACTIC KIDS

"THE FUTURE BELONGS TO OUR KIDS. WHAT WE THINK, SAY AND DO, THEY WILL REFLECT. IF THIS OCCURRENCE GLORIFIES GOD, ALL IS WELL."

We train our kids by being "models" for them. Even when logic and reason are catching up with their development, they do not want to be logical or reasonable. That is why respect and family order must be etched into the child before adulthood. I have found out that while I could control their activities in infancy, adolescence is the time to consider the effect that my domineering and demanding actions might have had on our children. I owe a lot to my father-in-law, Charlie Kalb. He tolerated my impatience with our children and never seemed to hold any of my child-rearing techniques against me, even though I now know that they were, for the most part, alien to his way of fathering. Charlie had an easy way with his children. He always wanted to show them a good time. One practice he taught me was to get the child involved in something fun and not to be so heavy on teaching the rules of the game. Try to enjoy the child and have fun even though the activity is not performed with scholarship ability. I was always trying to see if I had an All-American quarterback or a championship horsewoman in the group. Soon, time and Charlie convinced me to see that having fun and happiness with the child is more important than I ever considered. I always thought that I had to "teach" something. What I taught was how to frustrate the father and the children!! When I was a loving supporter, everyone did much better.

Mary Ann is like her dad. She believes in finding the next topic or activity to enjoy, but also like her mom and dad, she can work just as hard and just as long as I can. My idea of fun was adjusting until eleven o'clock each night! I am just now starting to loosen up! Mary Ann helped me by trying to get me involved in what interested the three kids. Even though I was not thrilled, I would go along and usually ended up having a great time. The reason for this, I believe, is because we are sharing family love, and that is ultimately one of the most important aspects of human life.

When our kids were small, we would try to explain the difference between what the medical doctors believed and what chiropractors believed. We carried this theme to the point of their once a week adjustments. Whenever they mentioned that one of their friends was very symptomatic – we tried not to allow them to use the word "sick" – and taking drugs, we would say something like, "It sure would be nice if your friends were taking adjustments and keeping up their immunity like you." As a side effect of this subtle approach, almost all of their grade school friends and teachers became patients of mine because of the kids' referrals! I often had the kids come to my patient lectures and every year we would take them to as many chiropractic meetings as possible. I told them that I hoped that they would all become chiropractors, but if they did not, we at least wanted them to graduate from college and find some vocation which helped people and the world in general. When they would say something like, "I want to be a baseball player," we would always respond with, "Great, you can be a baseball player AND a chiropractor."

We never hesitated to tell our three kids that chiropractors were different from medically trained people. We wanted them to understand that we were thankful that we were different. We always had more money than their friends, and until we moved to Atlanta, my kids thought that no one had more money, more cars, or bigger homes than we did! I was glad that Atlanta took the pressure off me!

As a teenager, I never wanted to drink! I finally figured out that I was scared I would become an alcoholic, as we had many in our family who were alcoholics. I never pushed this idea on the kids, but I told them that I was scared of alcohol. That is just the way it is with me. They can try it out, but I told them about the lives of alcoholics and gave them some statistics on alcoholism. I really believe that when your children become teenagers, you have no more real control over their lives. I have three teenagers now, and my prayers are that I may become more than a friend, hopefully their best friend, someday. I still direct and discipline them the best I know how, but I try to let them get involved in the decisions I have to make, especially the ones concerning their lives. I am trying to make a deal with each of them, but I do not know how far I am progressing. The deal is that I buy the cars, clothes, food, and everything else. All they have to do is to become chiropractors! That is not such a bad deal! I just cannot understand where they get the idea that they deserve all they get! My own childhood thoughts are returning through my kids – heaven forbid!

My advice for child rearing is to never complain in any way about your practice and try to be the model of a proud, positive, non-complaining, happy, loving, serving chiropractor. I am really convinced that God will do the rest.

When our kids were little, we were going through a vegetarian phase, so the kids were raised without meat for awhile. We have also fasted regularly for most of their lives, and they have fasted some, too. What we tried to accomplish by this discipline was to make them think about what they put into their mouths. We never gave them a vitamin pill or any other type of pill. In fact, the opposite is true. We reacted with great vehemence to pills of any sort. We tried to teach them that food which is bought or eaten out is not necessarily good food. We talked often about the fact that some kinds of prepared foods were even full of chemicals or just plain harmful. We did not buy soft drinks or junk food for years. I raised a large organic garden, and we ordered most of our other foods from health food stores. For a while, we even bought raw milk from one of my patients, and Mary Ann made our own butter. There were many times when we sat down to the table and ate a meal which had come only out of my garden or was made with raw products which we bought from other farmers in the area. Even though we are not so "pure" these days, it did accomplish one thing for me. I never take food for granted as before. This phase of my life made me stop and make a conscious decision as to the type, value, purity and amount of food my body needs. I eat junk food now and so do the kids, but at least we do not pretend to think it is good for us! The main objective here is that food, when we think of it, should not be based on what "tastes" good but on what IS good for the body. Innate has to use these foods and create our tissue cells with them. I look at our teenagers today and know that they will eat ANY type of food! I hope they picked up on some of our values and that they at least think about it more than their friends do. We have a rule at our house. Whenever we sit down to eat a meal together, we have to eat something raw first – salad, fruit, something that has not been cooked. Raw food has the most nutrition in it and that is where we need to focus our attention. We know that there are three foods we should limit, and those are fats, sugar and salt. Sugar is a detriment to the body, even though we all like the sweet stuff. Sugary foods lower the calcium in the blood for twenty-four hours.

Our rule is to eat all you want one day and then give Innate time to replenish the calcium over the next several days. When the kids were younger, I gave them two days to eat all their Halloween candy. What they could not eat, we threw out on the third day, with the hopes that the calcium level would come back. They soon found out that overindulging on sweets can cause symptoms! We do not have any other super-strict rules, except that junk food was considered to be a special treat when we ate out, or for something well done and not an every day nutritional standard. We still read the contents of the packaging labels, and we do not buy much junk food for home use. We used to only allow soft drinks and sweets to be eaten on weekends. I remember my old friend from Palmer, Frank Seubold, from Fort Smith, Arkansas. His parents were both chiropractors and very strict on nutrition. Frank always told the story that whenever his parents would go out of town, he and his brothers and sisters would always buy a case of soft drinks and overdose on them. I hope that we have not caused the opposite to be true in our family – that our kids feel it is okay to eat junk whenever they feel like it – but ultimately, one never knows until they become adults.

We talk about and use the word Innate very often, especially when we discuss symptoms with the kids. I also like to stress the amount of time and force needed within to bring about normal function and natural healing. The kids know that they must do things that will help Innate – more sleep, better nutrition, and regular adjustments – if they want to be well quickly. More is actually up to their innates, than to the chiropractor. That is the way it has been. I think that what Mary Ann and I have attempted to do is not to force our values down their throats, but to put emphasis on important matters. When the kids became teenagers, however, they remarked to me that most of my objections to things that they do seem to have a "health reason" behind them! Oh well!! Hopefully our kids' value system, when it comes to health, will be above average when compared to what their peers believe and practice.

Mary Ann and I try to give a lot of love to the kids. We kiss them a couple of times a day and tell them that we love them at least twice a day. The teens want to slow up on this routine I know because of the eventual need to leave the nest and become independent. But we keep up the "love bit" because even though they will be living away from home soon, we want them to know that we love and accept them with no strings attached. I believe that what I am doing most now for them is praying hard! As every parent with teenagers knows, they cannot listen except to their own consciences. Everyone must learn most from their own mistakes. Hopefully, the lessons will not be too severe.

Another practice I have begun with each child is buying them a little book on New Year's Day in which they are to write down their goals. At first, I helped them write down everything they could think of. We wrote about short and long range goals, and in the second year, we looked at what we wrote the year before. We wrote some more and subtracted some. Of course, the teens do not let me see their books anymore, but they still say that they do this goal setting each year at the New Year's time. I have done this myself for more than twenty-five years, and it is fun to look back at my life goals written down in retrospect.

Tommy goes to college next year and I plan on keeping up my own dad's practice of writing him every day while he is away at school. Dad got me into the writing habit, and I am thankful for it. Mom was too "practical" to let me phone home, so I had to write at least once a week – for money anyway.

Tommy played a couple of years of football in junior high school, and he got a lot out of it, like I felt I did. His real talent, though, lies with the books. He loves math and science and has told me many times that it is just there in his mind even before the teacher goes over the material. He is seventh out of more than four hundred students in his senior class. We are now encouraging him to get a scholarship. If he gets a full scholarship, I will buy him a new car. I think I will come out ahead on that deal. He wants to go to Palmer College after he gets his bachelor's of science degree. Amy and Jack are both above average students too, and I want them to see that I mean it when I say I will buy them a car if they get a scholarship. Believe me, they are looking, and I am saving up!!!

What I believe is important to begin in chiropractic college, is the changing of the medical model to the chiropractic model. The change is in attitude. The attitude one must seek to obtain is contrary to that of nearly everyone else in the world who does not know about the chiropractic principle.

Since the medical model looks at symptoms and conditions, the medical community talks about viruses, symptoms, and conditions as entities in themselves. They seek changes in or relief from these symptoms without focusing on the cause. It is a subtle thing not to even say you or your children are "sick." We try never to mention the word in our house. This is how it must be if you are looking at causes and focusing on corrections. I tried to get my children to come to their mom and me with the idea that they need an adjustment if they have a symptom. I would then go through my routine. This is how the script might go:

Child: "I need an adjustment."
Father: "Do you have a subluxation?"

Child:	"I think so."
Father:	"Where is it?"
Child:	"In my neck."
Father:	"What symptom is your subluxation causing?"
Child:	"Pain in my head."
Father:	"Is there pain in your neck?"
Child:	"My neck feels tight."
Father:	"Let me look at your neck. Here is the subluxation. This is causing your symptom (headache). I will adjust it. Innate will heal you. Is it better?"

This is a routine I have practiced over and over many times with my children. Mary Ann says, "Check my neck. I feel tension." When the kids would come home from school and say that a friend was home "sick" that day with the flu, I would ask what they thought about that. I would then ask if their friend got adjustments. Usually they did not have any idea, but constant focusing on the chiropractic model eventually made them think and eventually they referred many of their teachers and friends to my office for care! When I left Mississippi I had the principal of the elementary school and probably over one-half of the teachers there as patients.

As the kids grew up, I tried to keep them on a once a week check-up schedule so they were pretty symptom free. When I would see their resistance getting lower, I would question them in the following manner:

Father:	"You have low resistance today."
Child:	"Oh, my nose is running."
Father:	"You know what we call that symptom in chiropractic school?"
Child:	"No."

153

Father:	"We call it a 'hot'." Sometimes I would tell the Dr. Price story here.
Child:	"How can I get my resistance back up?"
Father:	"What does Innate need to raise your resistance back to normal?"
Child:	"I don't know."
Father:	"Think - subluxation? diet? rest? stress? Everything can't depend on the adjustments or what I do, so we will set up a plan of two check-ups a day, plenty of oranges and fluids. You need to get to bed early and wear warmer clothes."

If our goal for ourselves and our family is to get through life without a pill, then we have to look at the causes of symptoms and discipline ourselves to look for the "cracks" in our resistance and immunity. When you do this, then you will usually wind up thinking "I deserve this symptom" because you let yourself get subluxated, or run down.

I have written about all the good things I can think of, but when I reflect back on the kids, I know that there were a lot of days when I could have and should have done better. I hope this thought keeps me trying harder to be a better earthly father.

YOUR MENTORS

Everyone who is just starting out needs to have a "mentor," an experienced chiropractor who sets the example for you in your practice as well as in all of your professional life. Problems arise, however, when you put too much faith in him or her. I can compare this problem to my high school years, when I put every ounce of energy into my hot rod car. I expected it to bring me total happiness, to be my God and to deliver me into the dazzling field of male popularity. I expected young women to be screaming for my car and me! Instead, the car fell apart every time I dragged it, and I constantly put every dime I was saving for dates into the car instead. Finally, its three carburetors stuck, and the engine caught fire and melted the lead in the hood scoop, which put out the fire but destroyed the motor. When I finally sold the heap, I felt relieved, and I learned a lesson that no man could teach me. I learned that people and things are gifts for love and fun. You must expect "things" to let you down. They get scratched up, and friends reject you, but God, like Innate, is always constant. My mentors were numerous, even though I selected only the most successful chiropractors to pattern myself after. I thought they must have the answers and could help me accomplish great things. I also looked into their lives and saw mistakes, as well as ego-filled self-aggrandizement, written on a lot of their actions. What I wanted to do was accomplish what they had done, without making their mistakes. But I made plenty of mistakes even with their help. I wanted to believe that the system for practice that I constantly went over in my mind was going to work perfectly. But what these successful chiro-practors had were real life practices which worked. However, none of them used my "dream system." Thank goodness, I was smart enough not to believe in my own "genius," but to trust in their genius – the genius of experience. I watched and learned and even though I tried some of my dream system first, I soon discarded it and realized that my system had not been proven in the marketplace, and that is what counts in business.

I have mentioned some of my mentors before: Drs. Donald Pharoah, Herbert Himes, David Hughes, Orrin Hudson, Sr., John Blossom, Joe and Jack King, Charlie Boyd, Galen Price, Clay Thompson, Clarence Gonstead, J.J. Kehoe, Jim Parker, Sid Williams, Bill Harris, Arlan Fuhr and Mr. Greg Stanley. I owe these doctors a lot and want to publicly thank them – SO THANKEEE BOYS!!!

FOLLOW THE RULES

"IF YOU DON'T STAND FOR SOMETHING, YOU WILL FALL FOR ANYTHING."
Unknown

One of the efforts that can be counted during the "Pioneer Days" of chiropractic in Mississippi, was the enactment of the chiropractic licensing law in 1973. I wrote much of the final bill, and included the I.C.A. definition of chiropractic scope of practice in this bill. I helped the governor in Mississippi, through his aide, George Dale, set up the new chiropractic licensing board. When we first met, we elected our slate of officers, and I was the first executive secretary. It was Mary Ann's and my job to locate, qualify, grandfather, and license every chiropractor in the state of Mississippi. What a job!! The number of hours we spent with no salary was in the hundreds. To compound the process, the Medicare law was passed, and everyone had to take a test to qualify for Medicare. We also had our first examination for applicants for which to get prepared. At that time, there was no state assistance to our board. One lesson I learned very fast was to withstand the constant pressure to bend the rules and regulations for special people and special situations. I noticed that the twenty-two dollars and fifty cents per day which I made as a board member each day we met, qualified me as a state commissioner. I had to show an honest character. All of this activity was couched within the years of the largest practice we ever ran! We were young and dedicated, and our incessant belief that chiropractic is such a special profession kept us straight. What we learned, and not by mistakes, was to follow the rules. I had to tell close friends that their children had failed the examination. I had to turn down non-qualified friends from taking the exam. I went through much mental anguish from the pressure, because we wanted to help everyone. For all business and services, though, rules must be made and followed. Look closely at the moral choice. What is right? What is correct? That is what is important. It is difficult to tell you what people in decision making positions will do when bribed with money. In this matter, no one ever offered me money for a favor. Today, things are different. I do not know the number of embezzlements in different businesses, but none of them is worth the risk. I do not believe that there is "enough money" worth the risk of losing your license or serving a prison term.

My advice is aspire to be a leader in your state and national association and aspire to serve on a board of examiners. Once in a position of authority, work hard to be honest, with equality toward everyone, and you will be a blessing to your profession.

One bit of advice on holding a political position is BE PRE-PARED. Prepare for a diversion which takes away from your time in the office. Prepare for a loss of income; prepare for losing popularity and so called friends. But, do it anyway. Chiropractic needs you. I have no regrets.

GOTTA HAVE A HOBBY

"EIGHT HOURS WORK, EIGHT HOURS REST, EIGHT HOURS PLAY."
Old Masonic Axiom

Once the practice is rolling along fine, the diversions begin to follow the mind's idea of success. Some people require a hobby so compulsively that they have great success with their hobby and little success in their business. One of my friends, who is purported to be the best bass fisherman in the country, comes to mind. He is great at fishing but cannot seem to build a practice. The rule here for you new practitioners is to make sure that your hobbies follow rather than precede your success in practice. I know some students who concentrate more on their hobby and how it fits into the area where they want to practice than on picking out an area that would be more suitable for building a practice. Remember the advice about working hard the first ten years so the rest will be downhill. It is vital that you put all your energy into building your practice in the beginning. Know your peaks and your lows and never forget what got you to the top. You do not want to erode your dedication and lose control of your business. But once you have attained great success, you can do it again. The goal is to have as much fun and fluidity in your practice as possible so that it becomes your best hobby! At rest, you develop your pleasures.

I know several people who have many hobbies. They are always excited about the latest fad or gadget. One who comes to mind is very excitable and personable when he gets to talk about his latest hobby, but he has little to offer his patients in the way of chiropractic. He seems deeply committed to nothing!

I lived chiropractic twenty-four hours a day for the first three years in practice before I even found a hobby. That is right – I gotta have a hobby! I have always loved horses. My greatest childhood memories involved going to a barn owned by Devou Park, just outside of Covington, Kentucky. It was not far from our house, and the park superintendent, Vince Keller and his wife, Ethel, were my parents' best friends. Their daughter, Carol, and I would get to ride her horse every day. I still remember the smell of sweat grained in the leather tack. I became completely captured by the ethos of the barn and the horse. The manic feeling of being around the horse was always more than my senses could rationally handle. I have never been able to deal with the horse business in any way that resembled my average and customary actions in the business world. That is the only excuse I have for owning so many horses and never turning a great profit. When I got into the Tennessee Walking Horse business, I could afford a better blooded and bred horse. The excitement for me was in riding them. Whenever I feel that one thousand pounds of animal power swell under me, and the horse's response to the steel bit and spurs – it gives me a thrill just to write about it!

When I moved to Mississippi, I made sure that I brought my horse and trailer with me. Even though I did not have time for the horse, I made time, and Mary Ann would help me feed and care for it. I was aspiring to a great practice, and one day a friend told me I should sell the horse and get completely out of the business if I wanted to achieve my practice goals.

I argued with him that I could control my hobby and that it was no drain on me. A year later, however, I sold the horse. Within that year, I went from one hundred patients a day to two hundred patients a day, eventually averaging twelve hundred patient visits per week, and working all seven days. I must admit that I never knew the horse was holding me back. When I finally sold all the livestock, I felt free, but even though I got back in the horse business several years later, they never had the same possessiveness over me again. Now I do not even have to have a horse to ride, ALL the time! You may be like I was. You may not even realize that your hobbies possess you. Try getting away from them for one year. I guarantee that when you go back, they will not be the same.

I took up flying in the early 1970's, using the logical excuse that since I was traveling to Jackson, Mississippi, three times a week to lobby for our chiropractic licensing act, I could cut down considerably on my travel time by flying. I bought a fast plane – a Mooney Super 21 – but I still had to hire an instrument pilot to fly me to Jackson on the "weather" days. Have you ever noticed that pilots never call inclement weather "bad?" They only use casual words like "Weather is moving in!"

It might be a hurricane in actuality. Pilots learn an important rule about respecting their instruments, and the elements above all else. I later got out of my airplane hobby and submerged myself in chiropractic politics, horses, and organic gardening to supplement my already overloaded practice.

Probably my least expensive hobby has been writing music. I enjoy playing the piano, and God brings a song to me every once in a while. I invested in promoting a singer, however, and although we never got her a contract in Nashville, we were glad to help with her career. Otherwise, it has been a nice hobby that has brought me much enjoyment. I wanted our children to inherit my musical genes, so I hammered them to take lessons. They all would have liked to quit about half-way through, but the family rule (you can "take" anything of interest, but you cannot quit what you start) was in effect.

I do not believe that you can divide your interests, especially when you are first starting out. If you truly desire a goal, one that takes great sacrifice and effort, you must give up any hobby you have in order to attain it. If you are like me, you will think that the hobby is not pulling on you. But if you give up anything that possesses your conscious mind, thus creating singleness of purpose, you will also be free to give yourself the extra effort and time to move toward completing and perfecting your practice goals.

ON WITH THE CHIROPRACTIC MOVEMENT

The theory that for every action there is an equal reaction plays a significant part in the evolution of the chiropractic movement. In 1961, B.J. Palmer died, the American Chiropractors Association was formed, and a transition was in progress. There were many of us who were really caught up in the revolutionary mood. We were ready and willing to see that people everywhere were adjusted and made to understand the chiropractic principle. It was not the bone and nerve understanding that was most significant but rather the Palmer Law of Life – "What was health? Where does it originate? How can you correlate this law with the adjustment? How could we mount a national campaign to educate those in medicine, law, universities, etc. about chiropractic?" When I began practice, it was almost a sacred duty, as knowledgeable practitioners of this Law of Life, to adjust as many people in a day as possible and to continually tell our patients about our chiropractic health concepts. It was not only necessary, but more important it was RIGHT to be so obsessive with the volume practice in the early days. We were told by well-meaning friends that the world does not change this quickly and that it might take several lifetimes to see chiropractic gain its rightful place in the health field. We dismissed these thoughts as "negative" and kept on keeping on, adjusting as many people as possible and telling the story to anyone who would listen. After years of hard work, we found that flesh and blood does have limits after all. We could see two hundred patients a day for only so long before our frames became battered and torn. Like the time needed for Innate to heal our patients, it also takes time for the chiropractic profession to evolve. I am thankful to be able to look back and see what we did as positive to this evolution.

What we did in those days and what every new chiropractor needs to have is this extreme dedication, thus creating a new space in the world. This space is being filled now and the world is just beginning to see things our way. I believe the holistic movement of today is a direct outgrowth of the chiropractic movement of the 1960's and 1970's, even though the two were unrelated at the time. Our outgrowth even extended into the churches with all the Life Centers. Cigarettes are banned from advertising on television and next has to come alcohol and drugs. People are beginning to brag about not taking any medicine. There will be an effort to look seriously at our internal physical fitness as a pure bloodstream, natural immunity, and the importance of maintaining mechanical neuronal balance. A new dawn is approaching.

In the 1960s, the movement was toward the volume practice. This was the area of my greatest growth. Next the profession was changed when the first third-party pay system became a reality. This was brought about by our acceptance into Medicare and state insurance equality laws. This era in chiropractic brought much confusion to the volume practitioners, but it is a necessary part of our evolution since it was this era that established our unheard-of economic growth, recognition and prestige. Chiropractic colleges soon swelled with students. Federal accreditation ushered in the era of the highly educated chiropractor.

Now PPO's and HMO's are failing. The AIDS epidemic is escalating into a financial catastrophe for insurance companies.

National health insurance may indeed be just around the comer.

There will be a significant battle I believe for us to remain a separate and distinct profession. What we must do on a local level at this time is to group together in our practices and concentrate on becoming family doctors. We must spend all the necessary time to educate and speak to each patient as he brings in his children and family members for primary care. We must explain the myths of the drug theory and the importance of nutrition and monitoring the body systems as we correct subluxations in order to create a next generation with subluxation free, unpolluted bloodstreams and unaltered genetics. There must also be total faith in us to be the family's primary care doctor with emphasis on medical doctors for crisis situations only. The BIG challenge is to get through life without an aspirin or any other pill, to eat as organically as possible, and to be as physically fit as possible. Finally we must help people understand about Innate Intelligence and the importance of symptoms or warning signs that Innate gives them for health purposes. I also believe that chiropractic can have great input into natural living, coupled with psychological and religious understanding aimed at optimum mental health and spiritual growth.

In summary, every one of us needs to adjust as many people as possible, but now we must group together where the overhead and volume can be spread out and where the greater emphasis in the clinics can be on maintenance care, teaching, and "homework" for the patients. The era of physical, mental, and moral obligation will soon evolve. We need to be the bearers of the physical obligation and promote it to all with whom we come in contact. The time will come when it will be a crime to pollute the body with chemicals and other desecrating activities, as evidenced by substance abuse and drunk-driving laws. We need to become every bit as zealous as the mother who started Mothers Against Drunk Driving. It gets personal with us when we see our patients having unnecessary surgeries and taking unnecessary medications. By dealing with physical ailments naturally, we may even help people attain the physical purity necessary for spiritual growth. The new practitioner needs to spend the early years involved in the volume practice to really gain experience in knowing patients, developing adjusting techniques, and working with patients through all the phases of their care. Later we must become consultants and worldwide outreach activists. As you young chiropractors grow in knowledge and understanding of chiropractic and life, you need to become mentors. Remember anyone who has been on the battlefield brings back some experience and can become a mentor to some aspirant. Join in your chiropractic association, work hard, and pass it on to your children.

HOW TO VIEW YOURSELF ...
WORK AT IT!!!

MAKE YOUR OWN LIST.

I am a supreme optimist.
I am always on time or early.
I see my successes, and they make me positive to build more.
I always try to enjoy whatever I am doing.
I do not daydream about what might have been.
I do not think about what I did not do.
I study and learn more adjusting techniques each day.
I take better X-rays each day.
I get up early and jog three miles.
I never eat breakfast, only juices.
I try to eat only organic foods.
I try to drink only purified water.
I do not drink coffee or alcoholic drinks, and I do not smoke.
I try to eat a light lunch so I can work until 8:00 p.m.
I do not read newspapers except on Sunday and then I skim
    to see current events and look for ideas.
I read two or three books at a time.
I read a book on love and marriage several times a year.
I read spiritual books each day and pray for my spiritual
    growth.
I try not to watch television as often as I would like.
I turn off the sound and never watch a drug or booze com-
    mercial.

I have my office close enough to home where I can come home at noon when I want.

I take a twenty-minute nap every day.

I tell my wife and children that I love them at least every morning and night.

I work to overcome my laziness each day.

I examine old habits for possible elimination and improvement.

I know how to relax and I do this quite often.

I set my watch a few minutes fast so I am always ahead of time.

I write down my dreams and ideas day and night.

I hear new music in my head and I write it down and develop new songs.

I write down my lifetime goals, my yearly goals and daily objectives.

I always go in for night calls when it is a child.

I schedule my time on the calendar each month and make time for holidays.

I always schedule time for my wife, family and horses.

I read and study as well as take a technique seminar each year.

I give myself and family special rewards when important things have been accomplished.

I work smarter and harder.

I have confidence in my judgment of priorities and stick to them in spite of difficulties.

I get a mind fix on a project and muster all the determination and dedication I can to complete the job.

I use the ten-to-one rule on large purchases. I look at ten before I buy one.

I put ten percent of my income into a special account and never touch it (do not eat your children).

I concentrate on one thing at a time.

I try to stay with efforts that have long range benefits.

I keep pushing on items of necessity until complete.
I fast for twenty-four hours every week.
I pay myself first and save money every week.
I buy everyone everything I think I want to give them.
I buy a minimum of two tax free municipal bonds each year.
I try to have lots of time to rest on the weekends.
I attend chiropractic meetings at least four times per year.
I keep small talk out of my adjusting room conversation.
I am ready to serve whomever comes in my office today.
I am seeing booze, cigarettes and drug ads removed from television.
I regard my health as my supreme asset.
I look at food with the attitude of how organic it is and how it will help me.
I am trying to keep my weight constant and not overeat.
I continually ask myself "Have I done all I could do today?" and "What more could I do?"

You need to make a "New Me" list also. Write down your own affirmations. Concentrate on three of these a day for a week, then change to the next three on each Sunday night until the list is complete. Then repeat the process.

FINALE

God breathed the breath of life into us – Innate Intelligence. It is the creator of all our tissue cells. The work is connected with all order and function in the universe. To not give credit to Innate Intelligence for healing is to say that we are supreme egotists. Doctors should be humble and should know better!

To succeed in educating the public to the chiropractic way of looking at life seems simple. We must eyeball the innocent subluxated patients. They deserve our total love and concern for the few short moments of contact we have with them. We must adjust, educate, and continue to train others to do the same, patient, after patient, after patient ...

My Touch and Tell system helps to start this process.

Jack, Amy, Tom, Jr., Mary Ann and Dr. Tom Morgan

The "Morgan Manor" – Verona, Mississippi

171

*Family Clinic of Chiropractic
Verona, Mississippi – 1969*

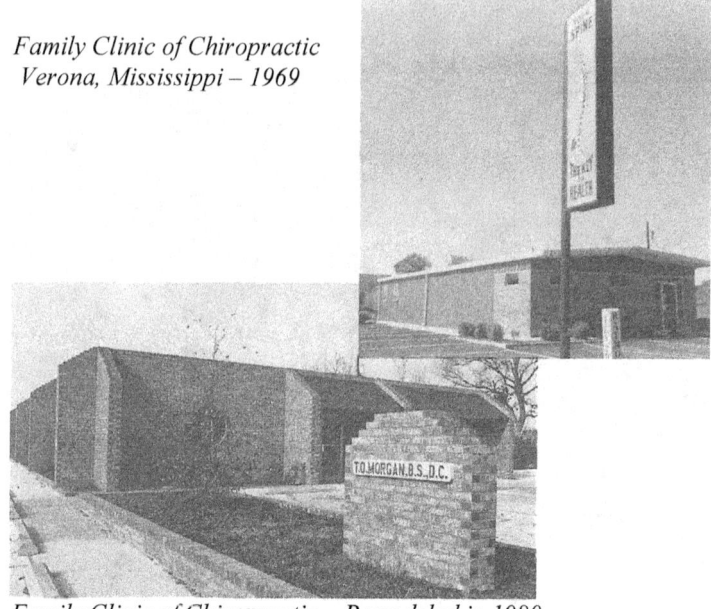

Family Clinic of Chiropractic – Remodeled in 1980

*Family Chiropractic Office
Austell, Georgia*

"Group Adjusting" Room

Mary Ann and Dr. Tom Morgan

"Run For Life"
1987 – Marietta, Ga.

Amy Morgan riding her famous Tennessee Walking Horse
"Great Big Country"

PART II

THE TOUCH AND TELL SYSTEM

I began this doctor-patient esoteric when I was in the student clinic at Palmer College of Chiropractic. I have refined and detailed this method over my twenty-five-plus years in private practice. It is a method that requires concentration and dedication. When achieved, it will do more to keep you "in tune" with your patients than any other procedure of which I know. We will begin with an overview of the procedure, and then we will go into specifics and actual patient-by-patient use of the data which is presented here.

INSPECTION

The touch and tell system relies on the doctor's perception of the entire patient and the subluxated spine through inspection, motion and static palpation, and leg testing. We will go through the procedure now, from beginning to end.

I am very interested in the center of gravity of the spine. I have found that changes in the A-P curves cause the most chronic problems and are also the most difficult to correct. Cervical hypolordosis and posterior weight bearing of the lumbar spine are most prevalent. These patients seen in the third decade of life, usually need regular adjustments for the rest of their lives. Complete corrections are possible, but the stabilization of the subluxation is most important.

When you begin, inspect the spine in a standing position. Note the A-P curves and the shoulder and hip levels. Bend the patient forward and observe the "rib hump." Then look for scoliosis and observe the motion in the three spinal regions. When the patient is thin and there is a hypolordosis in the cervical spine, he or she will usually be a nervous patient with gastric difficulties. If the patient is well nourished and the cervical hypolordosis is still present, then there are usually complaints of headaches or cervicallbrachial symptoms. A head tilt always indicates that the atlas is subluxated unless there is cervical muscle splinting. Laterality at the atlas causes the head to "tilt" to the opposite side.

While inspecting the spine visually, I begin to correlate my findings with the data that I have stored cortically. Then I begin my diagnosis. I do not ask the patient for symptoms at this time, and this is a vital key here. The symptoms, to be effective in my procedure, must always relate to the spine, with the subluxation being the cause. These must also be introduced to the patient's consciousness only at the specific time of my choosing, usually on the table during the static exam, while the patient is prone. Remember, we are in practice to correct causes, not symptoms.

A thin patient with a hypokyphosis in the thoracic spine will exhibit a very sluggish digestive system. Usually I tell the patient that he often loses his appetite and that his food tends to stay in the upper GI tract too long. Sometimes he may have symptoms of bloating and fullness for long periods of time. Scoliosis, particularly thoracolumbar scoliosis, has the most symptoms associated with thoracic pain. This, however, only occurs in the third decade of life and thereafter. Childhood scoliosis is usually very asymptomatic. Heavy patients with pendulous abdomens look way out of gravity balance. Usually, though, if it is a male patient, there are few back problems. I soon know if I can help this patient and I make it a point to do this, sending him on his way and instilling in him the concept of referring everyone he meets. I have found that it is important to channel the patient who gets well quickly so he can give you a testimonial and a referral. One word here – always tell the patient with chronic subluxations where the serious problem (subluxation) is located. He must understand that correction, not symptom relief, is needed. There is no "get well quick" path for chronic sufferers. After the patient completes the first or second phase of care, it is your duty to explain that the spine requires maintenance care once a week, twice a month – whatever you, as the doctor, decide – in order to stay healthy. It is most important that he complete his adjustment series.

Posterior weight bearing in the lumbar spine in thin patients is going to give you trouble, especially in older women. This does not mean that you will not get results or that these results will not be sufficient to keep the patient active. But you will have difficulties until you understand the case management procedures needed here.

Probably one of the most difficult concepts for new patients to understand is that within the body lies the intelligence to heal the condition. Next of importance is the subluxation and your adjustment of same. Aim all your patient education to satisfy these two points.

MOTION IN THE STANDING POSITION

First, have the patient forward bend. Observe the spine in motion, and watch the spinal muscles and palpate the hamstrings. It is very important to resolve the problem of tight hamstrings. You should start patient concern and exercises as soon as possible and urge the patient to continue the same for life. Tight hamstrings usually mean immobility problems, reoccurring low back pain, and vascular problems in the lower extremities. If the lumbar is rigid and immobile, you must decide right away if it is osseous or soft tissue rigidity. Osseous fixations in elderly patients indicate that you can help the patient right away. Exercise for the elderly is a key to rehabilitation and progressive chiropractic maintenance throughout life.

After forward bending, observe the movement on flexion and Kemp Tests. Localized fixation or inflammation of facets is usually indicated by pain being consistently in the same area upon movement. Usually you can correct this one area without difficulty. However, erratic pain on motion in different areas, even occasionally into the extremities, is confusing. You must then test the painful areas in other positions to determine if the pain is radiated or caused by specific lesions. Usually I gain a particular point of interest in the standing tests. Then I go to the supine and prone examinations to confirm my suspected conclusions. For example, if I find a patient who can forward bend to within several inches of the floor but cannot extend the lumbar spine and the pain is centered at the L5 area, I begin to suspect facet jamming, disk protrusion, and arthrosis associated with subluxation. I then test supine and prone to confirm my probable diagnosis.

PRONE EXAMINATION

This examination is essentially a chiropractic static palpation exam and it is at this time that I begin serious conclusions as to the subluxations and diagnosis. I always begin to suspect certain diagnoses, but I try to rule out all these suspicions with positive findings. On prone examination, I note leg length and Dierfield findings. I watch the leg flexion and look for facet jamming and pain. I watch the ilia for movement, and then I palpate the pelvis. The entire spine is palpated, and it is at this time more than at any other that I tell the patient every suspected subluxated area and the symptoms involved (the touch and tell system). This is when the patient's mind is partially shifted away from the main complaint and on to the spine, which is causing other conditions. I will go over this technique at the end of this chapter.

SUPINE EXAMINATION

The supine examination is primarily for orthopedic testing for low back problems. When I have a diminution in a reflex, I re-examine this reflex in several positions before I conclude.

SITTING EXAMINATION

I perform upper cervical motion tests, static tests, and examination of the upper extremities in this position. I pay particular attention to cervical compression, shoulder depression, and the scalenus anticus syndrome test. As stated before, it is important to notice head tilt. The atlas always goes high on the side of laterality, thus "tilting" the head over or down to the opposite side.

On each patient visit, I am concerned with the following: first to level the pelvic, the foundation. I tell my cervical patients that I must first level the foundation, so I can get the "roof" (or head and neck) on straight. I find the AS - ilium and PI - ilium. I test for internal and external rotation, pubic subluxations, trochanter rotation and sacrum laterality. The key is the sacrum. I force the legs up to the hips (prone) to check for facet jamming and anterior L5. Next I am very concerned with the transition vertebrae (L5, L4, T12, T11, T8, T6, T1, C5, and of course, the axis and atlas). I still believe the atlas moves inferior instead of finding so many occiput subluxations. Also, I now believe, with isolation testing, that the scapular/arm pattern, AC joints and knees are important in the correction of any misalignment or fixation. It is very interesting, after hard bone moving for over twenty years, to do more and more, with less force and high speed. That is one of the reasons why I use Activator Methods exclusively.

INSTRUMENTATION

I used the NCM at Palmer and a neurocalograph in my practice for five years on every patient. I have also used a nervoscope, and I now rely on the Activator leg testing system. I have sat through classes on heat-reading instrumentation until I am totally confused! What I am trying to say is that after all these years of using an instrument, the only consistent thing – and consistency is a problem – is that a "reading" in an area may mean a "problem" somewhere. It is not always present in the area with the reading. I recommend that all students and new doctors use an instrument in the beginning, even if they do not understand the readings or even if they become frustrated with the instrument. The reason for this is that the discipline causes you to pay particular attention to the most important component of the subluxation complex – the neuronal component. After using the instrument on many patients, I find that the cold reading on the transverse process of the atlas is consistent with atlas laterality, particularly in children. I used the DTG like the old chirometer. I now feel, after learning all the sixty-plus isolation tests in Activator Methods, that I can locate the subluxations more specifically. This reflex testing is like asking Innate to "fire" the reflexes and I watch the reactive leg movements. After the adjustment, the legs balance.

SYMPTOMS AND VERTEBRAL LEVELS

You may note that the symptoms do not always correspond to the expected Meric anatomy. I believe that the vast predisposing spinal nerve branches and integration of the sympathetic and parasympathetic systems cause this to be true. Let us look at some spine levels, and we will discuss their ramifications.

OCCIPUT SUBLUXATION

When there are taut and tender fibers along the inferior nucal line of the occiput and the atlas and axis are not involved, I tell the patient that there are vascular changes in the head. If the pressure is more right than left, I ask if there is skiminess over the eyes. There are always occipital headaches and they will usually happen when the patient first arises. They originate in the occiput and become cluster headaches in the daytime, including pain with the entrance of light. I always do the Georges Test on every new patient. Ischemic changes do occur in this level of subluxation and the doctor must use caution with rotating and adjusting. The technique I used to use was a modified Gonstead move, prone. I now use the activator. The head is tilted and never rotated or used as a lever. The point to remember on correction is that the occiput/condyles need only be aligned on the atlas right to left or left to right. Pay particular attention to the angle of the condyles when adjusting.

183

ATLAS SUBLUXATION

First you need to know if the pressure is only on the atlas. The static point for this determination is the transverse process (TP). The point of pressure is normally right on the far lateral tip of the TP. If there is one side that palpates pressure, then I ask the patient if his eye muscles on the same side exhibit a tremor. Usually these are intrinsic muscle tremors, and the patient will remark that he feels the eye twitch, but he cannot see it when he looks in the mirror. If the pressure point on the tip is great and the transverse is anterior, I tell the patient that he does not have headaches very often, but when he does have one, he remembers it for a long time (migraine). This anteriority will cause the eustachian tube to exhibit pressure sensations, and I also relate this to the patient. Tension on the TP exhibits sharp neuralgic type pain on the parietal area on the same side. This pain is an instant, sharp, severe pain. The patient remembers these symptoms, and when I find these points, I tell them that I can correct the cause of these symptoms. Sometimes I even say I can help "cure" these problems!

I believe that the occiputalatlantaxial area is the most important area to keep checked and adjusted. If the patient has severe pressure in this area, I try to educate him regarding the seriousness of his subluxation and make sure that he makes this area a priority in the health care maintenance schedule.

The most important correction to make of the atlas listing is the laterality. While I was a state board examiner for twelve years, the most consistent technique failure I observed was the set up and correction of atlas laterality. Everyone wanted to use the head as a lever and rotate the upper cervical area so that he could hear audibles. At best, these doctors could only correct rotation. If you see laterality on X-ray and want to be sure of correction, I recommend that you adjust right to left or visa versa with minimal rotation of the area, using diversified technique. My special move is to have the patient lie prone with the table at a forty-five-degree angle, I tuck the chin down and tilt the head toward the side of the listing, while thrusting straight laterally with my double jointed thumb. Today, however, I use the activator. I feel that it is an extension of my hand, and the levels of energy the instrument uses makes the correction fast, efficient, and extremely safe. If the atlas is lateral on the condyles and the cervical scoliosis is on the same side, the adjustment will stabilize completely, and you can usually correct the subluxation in a minimum amount of time. However, if the axis spinus is to the opposite side of atlas laterality and the scoliosis is opposite or absent, you have a tough correction to make. If you have a problem, do not hesitate to refer these patients out to upper cervical practitioners if necessary. These chiropractors spend their entire professional lives correcting this subluxation and are very adept at it.

A very important note on C1 is the inferiority subluxation. If the atlas palpates inferior, usually from a compression injury, there is going to be an extremely nervous patient. You will visualize a narrow posterior archlocciputal space. I tell this patient that I have located what is causing him to be so nervous and unable to sleep. I tell him that it is inside nervousness, not mental, caused by the subluxation of C1. Sometimes patients can relate to outside versus inside tension. There is no way to tell how many depressed patients chiropractors have helped and how many suicides have been thwarted because of this atlas correction. Keep up the "life releasing" doctors. God blesses your great undertaking.

AXIS SUBLUXATION

This is the easiest area in which to locate symptoms or subluxations. The pressure point is on the lamina pedicle junction, and if the spinus is rotated to the same side as body rotation, tell the patient that this subluxation is causing those tension headaches on the same side, usually frontal in nature. Also, if the atlas is exhibiting the same amount of pressure as the axis on the same side, you can tell the patient that this subluxation is causing his sinus problems and that his head always stops up on the same side and drains on the opposite side. This may include upper respiratory symptoms, but usually there is a variable on chronic upper respiratory problems.

I have found that the axis is also the cause of the "crick" or muscle splinting when the anterior paravertebral muscle groups are involved. When the SCM muscle splints (i.e. torticollis), it is always atlas/axis to the same side. The axis is the student's "dream adjustment" because you can usually move it with any contact and any thrust. So be my guest and use any move you like! Yes, you must use the head as a lever and rotate the axis somewhat when you adjust. This is the only cervical vertebra that I rotate when I adjust by hand. Using the activator, I thrust toward the nose without rotation. With geriatric patients, a superior axis spinus is often involved with vertigo (vertebral basilar syndrome). If the patient has a posterior "crick," usually it involves the trapezius muscles and a C5-6 subluxation.

VARIABLES

When you find "cord" pressure in the upper cervical subluxation, be sure to explain this serious subluxation to the patient. If I were a patient and had this problem, I would be thankful that a chiropractor took the time to explain its complexities and set up an appropriate adjustment schedule. Usually this patient must come regularly for life.

Variables occur when the condyles are one way and/or the atlas and axis subluxate opposite to each other. Variables can get very confusing and also very serious. They are noted primarily on X-ray and can cause such "dread" diseases as epilepsy, diabetes, psychosis, learning disabilities, CVSs, arythmias, hypertension, immune disorders and many other related conditions. Their pressure points are also variable and not constant enough for me to put into an overview. I will, however, now give a simplistic overview of the consistent pressure points by which you can begin to identify certain conditions with a high degree of accuracy.

THIRD CERVICAL SUBLUXATION

The pressure point for C3 is the transverse process. Palpate the TP bilaterally and when there is pressure on one side, you can tell the patient that there is an unusual subluxation here. You will see very few. The lateral cervical X-ray will confirm posteriority along with hypolordosis. This subluxation will exhibit weird and unusual symptoms such as headaches in a circle on the top of the skull, tremors in the upper extremities of elderly patients, patches of alopecia in the back of the head, excessive warts on the upper extremities of adolescents, and paresthesia of the lips. When I see these symptoms, I begin to suspect C3 and so should you. I adjust a posterior C3 with the patient lying prone. I use the web between the thumb and first finger and I thrust P-A without the drop headpiece. Listen for audibles. The test with the activator has also proven conclusive.

FOURTH CERVICAL SUBLUXATION

The pressure point for C4 is anterior to the TP almost on the vertebra body. You must use caution to "touch" for these pressure points and not use heavy palpation. Watch the carotids and anterior ligaments. This is the throat vertebra. When you find pressure in this area on either or both sides, you can tell the parent that his child has been having frequent low resistance in the throat area, causing sore throats. You can then examine the tonsils for hypertrophy and scarring which indicate reoccurring infections. Remember tonsilar hypertrophy will not resolve. Keep children with this problem under a regular care program to keep their resistance at a maximum. By watching the child's subluxation and nutrition, you can help Innate keep the throat infection down, and the child's throat will finally grow to accommodate the large tonsils. "Save those tonsils" has been a motto of chiropractors for many years so do not miss the chance to help these young people. When you find the pressure in adults you can look for "neurological" sore throats as well as infections. The cause is the same – subluxation.

My pet move is done in the prone position. There is usually only a lateral wedge here, and you do not have to worry about posteriority. Remember, I said try not to rotate the cervical spine while adjusting. You can get away with it on the young patients, but I do not believe that you do the spine well to torque the disk. Do not turn the head past a ten or twenty degree "tilt". Never pick up the face and turn it ninety degrees except when adjusting C4. The only time I ever turn the head ninety degrees and "lock" is when adjusting C4. The contact point is as far anterior as possible on the body. The thrust is a "lift" from inferior to superior and you will feel the C4 "set" into position. You must use caution here because you are close to the larynx, pharnyx, and the carotids, and the patient must totally relax the musculature while you give an arching, thrusting "lift" move. I usually use the second joint of the index finger as my contact point. The underside of the contact finger is used while standing superior. If the contact is on the right of C4, you will stand slightly anterior and use the left index finger. Today, I get the same results adjusting into the facet angle with the activator.

FIFTH AND SIXTH CERVICAL SUBLUXATIONS

C5 is a very important vertebra to keep clear. The posteriority in this area must be corrected. The area here that I find to be so important is the cervical lymph chain. I was taught at Palmer by Dr. Pharoah in the early sixties to always palpate the cervical chain in the sitting position on every child. You can tell the resistance of the child by examining and following the progress of the cervical lymph chain. Large, soft nodes indicate recent low resistance and acute infection. As the nodes enlarge, you will be able to tell the parent when to expect a fever which will increase the lymph activity and reduce the gland size as it reduces the infection. This will tell you to stay close to the child or adult because with fevers, you must adjust frequently until it stabilizes. Density of the glands will indicate long-standing, low infection and immunological weakness. These cases must have regular adjustments with dietary considerations. Only after regular care for a year or two will you see dense, calcified nodes resolve. As you know, immunology in medicine is a relatively new field, and it has only been twenty years or so since the discovery was made that the lymph system is the master control system of all immunological activities. So respect the C5 subluxation and the immune systems at this level.

C6 is not as prevalent a subluxation as C5. However, C5 and C6 are the anterior points of the lordosis and need to be put as close to a normal position as possible. I use the Kla-Gro plotter to mark the 17 centimeter arch, and I am very emphatic to patients when having them follow the series of adjustments designed to correct the hypolordosis and subluxation complex.

The weight-bearing changes in the hypolordosis cause the articular facets to erode at a great speed because of the jamming effect of the hypolordosis. When you see density changes on X-ray at this level, do not become discouraged about the degree of correction and prognosis. I have even seen spurs absorb following correction.

Tell the patient with the hypolordosis and the C5-6 subluxation that this is what is causing them to have those "cricks" in the neck as well as paresthesia in the upper extremities. C5-6 is the radial nerve level, and I always trace the nerve down the arm. Usually I can tell if the first two fingers and thumb are involved with radial nerve tracing. You should be able to tell the patient which arm is affected. I use various P-A moves in this area, while being careful not to torque the disk. Please do not forget to tell the patient that this subluxation is causing the crepitation they have been hearing in their neck.

SEVENTH CERVICAL SUBLUXATION

This is the subluxation that I relate to AC problems (bursitis, tendonitis, and shoulder girdle splinting). The pressure point is the spinus process and it will be tender on static palpation. Pay attention to elongated cervical ribs and hypolordosis involving this subluxation. The stiffness and soreness in the traps and brachial levels are an indication of this subluxation. Tell the patient that you can reduce this aching area with the adjustment. Also palpate the thyroid for hypertrophy when C7 is subluxated.

FIRST THORACIC SUBLUXATION

T1 is the ulna nerve area that I find affected the most. Tell the patient with this subluxation that the little finger and the ring fingers are sometimes numb because of this subluxation. The patients probably will not know what a subluxation is at this point, but that is the "mystery" about which you want them to learn. Once in a while, I will find the TP pressure point extremely posterior bilaterally, and when I find this, I tell the patient that he has had pain in the clavicularsternum articulation. The activator test is conclusive.

SECOND THORACIC SUBLUXATION

T2 is always an indication of chest pain. When I find the high TP very tender, I tell the patient that this subluxation, as I goad the tender TP, is causing the sharp pains in the chest over the ribs. Notice that I said "ribs," not "heart." I explain that the sharp pain which the patient has been feeling is caused from the subluxation and that I can help correct it. When there is arythmia associated with the chest pain, usually you must adjust the atlas along with T2.

THIRD THORACIC SUBLUXATION

The pressure point is on the TP, and the symptoms are primarily concerned with the bronchials and the lungs. I can tell in a child if there is repeated bronchial problems or asthma. As in all pressure points, if you sense the problem from the subluxation, ask the patient about the condition. If you are not sure, merely tell the patient that this nerve inervates the bronchial area. Ask if he has bronchitis very often or has a history of asthma. When I find a pressure point, I am insistent about finding out the symptoms involved with the subluxation. So I stay with the questioning until I can relate to what I have found. I do not "scare" the patient, but I merely "fish" for what symptoms are associated with the subluxation. Store this information for another time.

In the upper thoracic muscles, particularly in the trapezius, you find much stress and splinting. Taut and tender fibers indicate postural deficits and subluxations. When you find pressure points on the spinuses of T1, 2, and 3, tell the patient that he has burning and pain in these muscles and that you can resolve this problem for them.

FOURTH, FIFTH, AND SIXTH THORACIC SUBLUXATIONS

When these vertebrae are in an anterior position (hypoky-phosis), you can tell the patient that he often loses his appetite and food tends to stay in the stomach too long, making him feel bloated and full. Look for the Tums on the counter next to his glasses, and do not miss the chance to tell him how much aluminum is in them and how aluminum is a dangerous metal isolated in arthritic joints. Now the drug companies are pushing Tums for calcium, while the osteoporosis scare is on. The drug companies!! UGH!! Who will pay for all their blood pollution?

If these vertebrae are posterior and there is a pressure point on the spinus, then there is usually hyperacidity and gas. Also this is usually an overweight patient, which indicates that he will eat constantly from anxiety. You must watch this area on those patients where the sympathetic/parasympathetic crossover is suspected. We will discuss my thoughts on this at the end of the chapter. This area is usually a compensation so you will have to adjust the subluxation above and below. T6 is the major subluxation.

SEVENTH, EIGHTH, AND NINTH THORACIC SUBLUXATIONS

When there is pressure on the TP, I tell the patient that I can correct the subluxation which is causing him to be tired and have that "rundown" feeling. These patients will go to bed tired and get up tired. The problem, I believe, is the conversion of sugar into glycogen in the liver which can correct itself once the subluxation is corrected. T8 is the major.

TENTH THORACIC SUBLUXATION

This area is like the lower cervical area, inasmuch as the anterior weight bearing must be present. When there is a subluxation in this area, there is a postural deficit also. Then the patient must be instructed about maintaining the proper adjustment correction schedule. The pressure point is the spinus process, and the symptoms involved are electrolyte problems (mainly retention). I usually tell the patient that this subluxation is causing them to have fluid, swelling and retention. This area primarily involves the adrenals.

ELEVENTH AND TWELFTH THORACIC SUBLUXATIONS

This is the nephric area and a very significant area for subluxations. The transverse processes will palpate hard and rigid. Usually this rigidity is caused from kidney abuse, (trauma as well as poor nutrition) and weight bearing, as this is a transitional area. Look for this to occur in heavy drinkers, soft drink and iced tea addicts. I usually tell the patient that he is having aching in this area of the spine and that we will have to see what is causing it. During the report of findings, on the second visit when there is a wedge on X-ray, I ask about his fluid intake and tell him about the importance of normal kidney function. If you have a water distiller, like I have used for fifteen years now, and you find a lot of limestone and canselus material collecting in its boiler, you will want your patients to also consider using one. If the pressure point is on the TP, there is possibly a history of calculi. I have never had a patient with repeated caculi episodes that did not become much improved with a regular adjustment program. Be sure to go after these patients with stones; for while medicine keeps inventing new technology for calculi detonation, the cause (subluxation) is overlooked, and this is exactly what we can help.

This is also the subluxation involved in hypertension. I usually adjust this area and not the upper cervicals or vice versa when the symptom is chronic hypertension. You can do much more for this type of patient than any drug can do. I ask the hesitant patient, who fears ever coming off of the blood pressure medication, if the medical doctor had told them about the side effects of his medication. Usually the doctor has not told them anything! So, let this patient see your physician's desk reference and circle "impotence" for the men. Even medical doctors will not take this drug! I have had patients depend on the adjustment and diet to control their blood pressure for years with much success. You must design your health care programs for these patients so that they can understand that there is indeed an alternative to drugs. I adjust with the activator now, but I used to get audibles on the knee chest table when adjusting these vertebrae.

FIRST AND SECOND LUMBAR SUBLUXATIONS

Most of the unidentified abdominal complaints are in this area. When I examine a young patient and the pressure point is on the TP on one side, I tell the patient that the subluxation here is causing the pain in his side when he runs. Problems involving the gut area are harder to pick up. However, when the appendix has been "hot," I find the entire segment posterior, very rigid, and desperately in need of an adjustment.

THIRD LUMBAR SUBLUXATION

When I find pain and pressure on the spinus of L3, I tell the male that this is causing pain to radiate in the spermatic cord area and testicle on the side of body rotation. Usually they have been misdiagnosed by the medical doctor as having prostatitis, and the patient has much concern that the symptoms are still present. Pressure on one TP in females indicates ovarian problems, and usually there will be cramps and difficulty every other month when the subluxated side (open side of the wedge) is involved with ovulation. I have seen disk lesions in this area, and the symptoms involve pain in the area of the ischium bones. Sometimes the patient cannot sit on the ischium very well. Also, there is usually some pain along the inferior gluteal folds. This is caused by the pressure on the caudia. I use activator now, but have gotten good results with modified disk traction on these cases and adjust L3 on a drop table on exhalation.

FOURTH LUMBAR SUBLUXATION

The pressure point will be on the spinus and the female will always have bladder pressure and repeated infections of the UG tract. In the fifth and sixth decade of life, I always tell the patient that this subluxation is causing the bladder to "leak" when they laugh or cough (incompetence). Teenagers can have this symptom with an L4 subluxation, too. Men have prostate and erection problems. You can help these patients tremendously. If the pressure point is on the TP only, then there is pain in the knees. Even the elderly with hypertrophic knees can be helped. I have had patients come in for more than ten years with big hypertrophic knees and swinging gaits, yet still receive much help. I believe that Innate can arrest this knee destruction with regular adjustments. You can even save a lot of patients from having to have complete prosthesis of the knee if you will adjust them every week for the rest of their lives.

FIFTH LUMBAR, SACRUM, AND PELVIS SUBLUXATIONS

I put these bones together because of the importance of this area and the significant technique I use for telling the patient what the subluxation is causing. First of all, the sacrum is the key. It must be level and completely mobile. When you find that the body of L5 is rotated to the same side as the posterior sacrum, you have an easy case to fix. Usually this will occur with overstrained muscles or ligaments. Even in severe antalgic patients in great pain, you can tell the patient that his condition is very painful but not serious. I flex the legs to the buttocks on the leg check and look for sacral movement and facet jamming at L5. When I find this, I suspect posterior weight bearing in the lumbars. This is one of the most important postural deficits to correct.

Women with severe anterior tilt of the pelvis will have varicosities. The side of the greater subluxation will cause one leg to be worse than the other. Young pregnant patients with this subluxation can develop varicose veins practically overnight during the second trimester. Adjust these patients up to the two hundred and eightieth day!

A simple PUN on one side with a stable L5 will have only cramps in the lower legs and you can tell patients this on examination. The pressure point is in the SI joint on the affected side. When the body of L5 is rotated opposite to the posterior sacrum, you have a very difficult case. I always tell patients with a severe posterior apex that they have had an injury to the tailbone, and that is why it goes numb when they sit. Usually this is also the cause of their "nagging" back. If the sacrum is anteriorly fixed between the ilia, then there are hemorrhoids involved. After the X-rays and motion tests, I group this area into the following categories in my mind for diagnosis and patient management:

Subluxation causing:

1.   Facet arthrosis, jamming, or inflammation
2.   Disk protrusion, right, left, or medial
3.   Sprains and strains
4.   Inflammatory joints and degenerative disk disease

5. Mechanical deficits

I use the activator and believe in the pelvic correction. I have also used the Thompson Table prone and supine. I do not use any "rolls" or side moves, because as I mentioned before, I do not like to torque the disk. I use the side moves only to leverage the back on severe splinting, and I do this only to reduce the spasms. Dr. Gonstead once told me in private that if he could get every chiropractor to learn to clear out the laterality of atlas, the posteriority of the lower cervicals and the sacrum, they could get ninety percent consistent results. I believe that this is true. The other ten percent is in the "bag of tricks" which you have learned from experience.

GENERAL NOTES

There is a very small percentage of cases which you cannot adjust into both the sympathetic and parasympathetic systems. This crossover will cause unfavorable reactions to the adjustments. After twenty years, I can pick some of these cases out upon entrance, but I miss some, too. So when the patient is having weird symptoms following the third or fourth adjustment and you are sure that it is not because you have induced too much technique, then you usually have a sympathetic case, where you can adjust the upper cervical and pelvis only; or a parasympathetic case, where you adjust the subluxations from C6 to L4. I have been a full-spine adjuster for more than twenty-five years, and I always find that the more specific you become – usually find not more than two or three major subluxations on each patient, – the better technician and chiropractor you become. The chiropractors who think that they must mobilize every segment in any way, have not taken time to be specific. I still take technique courses every year, but am extremely cautious to watch the technique teachers as they have a tendency to want to "sell" themselves and the fact that their technique is "absolute." Every new technique I learn, I test it to my proven palpation skills, thus developing my own "bag of tricks." Through the years I have stored away a lot of technique tricks in my "bag." When I learn a new technique, I never throw the bag away and start something totally new just to try it out. Integration is the key here.

There has been one exception. It took my good friend, Dave Hughes, two years to get me to an activator seminar. Dave is one-hundred percent activator and even has several isolation tests named after him. When I heard the live-animal study data that Dr. Fuhr presented, I finally understood the mechantor-receptor mechanisms and began to understand how a low force technique really worked. For the first time, I could correlate my "touch and tell" analysis with Dr. Fuhr's isolation tests. We were well into the ninety percent compatibility range. I am impressed. I worked hard studying Fuhr's videos every night until I now know every test on the basic and advanced work. Dr. Fuhr admits to borrowing from all the techniques using leg testing and credit is due to these men who labored long and hard on the different techniques themselves. Some of these are Drs. Van Rumpt, DeJarnette, Goodheardt, and others. I was so satisfied with the hard bone moving, that I just could not take the time to understand the low force techniques until recently. Today, I am concentrating on using less force to achieve more results. My results are, in fact, better. My post X-rays are better. I have been inspired!

Activator has made me a better chiropractor! I still touch and tell, as I want to lay my hands on the subluxations, and I post same after the isolation tests and adjustment. I recommend activator to everyone now. Even if you prefer the high force techniques, activator can only increase your subluxation detection and correction. What I believe we are doing when we watch the mechano-receptors fire the reflex (and shorten the leg) is in actuality asking Innate where the subluxation is and where it is not. Nothing else can give this data to the chiropractor today.

THE TOUCH AND TELL SYSTEM
OVERVIEW

New patients fill out their entrance history with a small space for the chief complaint. Then they are placed in an adjusting room. I greet the patient, discuss very briefly the chief complaint, and right away begin telling him what I am going to do. I am not interested in being overly friendly and beginning a long conversation about his complaints. I am interested in the doctor-patient bond that can only come about as I pick up the feedback on this procedure. Usually, for me the bond solidifies after I come back into the adjusting room with the X-rays and the first report. At this time, I feel that I know the subluxation and the patient's condition. I also have a good idea of what it is going to take to correct this condition and help the patient. When I feel this bond, there is a trust that develops and the patient knows in his heart that I have help for him. Innate does the healing and I do the adjusting. It is the great work that God gave me to do, so I am thankful.

I explain to the patient that I am going to first give the entrance examination. I say something like "Come up to the table. You have been to a chiropractor before, so you must know how to 'ride' one of these tables." Then I tell him that I want to begin with the preliminary exam to determine where the cause of his problem is and where I need to X-ray. I then put the patient down on the table, and without asking any questions, I make sure that I locate the exact point of pain, cause of pain, and any other information that I can give the patient concerning his chief complaint. In other words, I want to tell him whether this condition is reoccurring, chronic, or acute; into what areas it is radiating, etc. I actually relate all the symptoms to him that he would have told me face to face. The reason I do this while the patient is face down, is because I want him to know that I can tell where he is hurting and that these symptoms are related to one mysterious word – SUBLUXATION. Next, I explain that I am going to examine all the joints and nerves in the spine. I go to the cervical spine, for instance, and start asking him if he knows how many bones are in the neck. Along with this information on the spinal nerves, I also begin to look for pressure points. I "touch and tell" the patient what symptoms he has and what is causing them. Many times he thinks that I am a "mind reader" or that I have talked with someone who knows all his "deep dark secrets!" I am on the POSITIVE side of the symptoms at this time, and this is where you and I want to stay.

As I find pressure points, I draw on all my experience to relate the symptoms to his subluxations. Hopefully then, the patient's mind starts relating all the symptoms to a cause in the spine. I then get him off the table and write down what we have just found. I may ask him more about his "other conditions." Next, we go to the X-ray room. After the X-rays, I have Mary Ann do the motion tests as well as the orthopedic and neurological tests indicated. After the X-rays are out of the processor, I wait until I feel that I have something positive to tell the patient about his subluxations being the cause of his condition. Then I meet him again and give him my first report. If the patient needs acute care, I usually adjust him then. Time is always a factor.

On the second visit, I enter the room and begin to explain the routine adjustment procedure for the patient's benefit. I put him down on the table first. You see, I think it is important to establish in the patient's mind the exact procedure to follow on each office visit. Many times, I will explain that we are not medical doctors, and our procedures are different. What I want to do on every visit is to establish in his mind that the subluxation CAUSES and the adjustment CORRECTS. He gets used to not talking to me first, and I get used to talking to him while he is on the adjusting table and I am examining the spine. This way, my concentration is on the subluxation and what it is causing. I talk about what I am doing throughout the adjustment. When I am finished, he gets up, and I show the X-rays, give reports, or just visit with him for a while. It is most important, though, to keep your procedures consistent. As the patient progresses through the years, you keep reading the subluxations and telling him what nerves are involved, what organs are involved, what symptoms he is experiencing, and how you can help him. When you are able to tell him his symptoms by examining his spine, you will have referrals like I have had, where the patient lists on his case history under chief complaint "You tell me." When I see this, I know that one of my patients has told this person that I can find the cause of any problem in the spine.

I believe the purpose of the "Touch and Tell System" is to keep the patient from dumping the symptoms on me. I cannot really do anything about the negativity that the symptoms present, and it does not improve my skills. So I turn the symptoms into something positive when I discuss them through location and correction of spinal subluxations. I use the negative symptoms for a positive benefit in this way. Symptoms are very important to people. The medical doctors and the drug companies have made sure of this. We have to use these symptoms in a positive way. This system evolves itself after awhile, to the point of having the subluxations stabilize and the patient becomes "clear." One purpose for using this system is to ask the patient how he is feeling only when you know for sure that he is better and will relate all symptoms to his subluxations.

FINALE

"PAIN IS INEVITABLE, BUT DISCOURAGEMENT IS OPTIONAL."

Unknown

I said in the beginning of this book that I wanted to share my success in a high volume practice. I hope that you have felt through the printed word the wonderful time we have had in chiropractic as well as the years of constant practice, always trying to do what is right to help patients. I hope you can feel within yourself a desire to be the best chiropractor you can possibly be, to work within the profession, and to pass your knowledge and understanding on to the next generation.

I think that it is important to improve and go forward, by using hindsight (the perfect science) to help you avoid making the same mistakes again. Chiropractic has come a long way since I first entered Palmer College in 1960. We still have much to do and much to learn. Some of you reading this will see the entire profession change more in a decade than it has changed in ninety-five years. Some things, however, will never change. Success is one of these. The technology may vary, but the rules will be the same. I hope that I have explained some of these rules in this book. Some will push through their weaknesses and reach that sublime, unfettered position of peaking out in a practice situation reached only by a few. So, set your sights. A firm, quiet resolve must be first. Then a lot of prayer and work must follow. The blessings you receive from God are like grace – an undeserved promotion. They will make you humble but truly blessed and truly promoted.

Continue following the inspirational pathway to chiropractic success in Dr. Morgan's Volume Practice II!!!

Over 430 pages of his lifestyle of success, advice and practice building tips!!!

Order it today!!!!